50 Walks in
BERKSHIRE &
BUCKINGHAMSHIRE

First published 2002
Researched and written by Nick Channer

Produced by AA Publishing
© Automobile Association Developments Limited 2002
Illustrations © Automobile Association Developments Limited 2002

Published by AA Publishing (a trading name of Automobile
Association Developments Limited, whose registered office is
Millstream, Maidenhead, Windsor, SL4 5GD;
registered number 1878835). A00905

Ordnance Survey® This product includes mapping data licensed from
Ordnance Survey® with the permission of the
Controller of Her Majesty's Stationery Office.
© Crown copyright 2002. All rights reserved. Licence number 399221

ISBN 0 7495 3334 X

A CIP catalogue record for this book is available
from the British Library.

The contents of this book are believed correct at the time of printing.
Nevertheless, the publishers cannot be held responsible for any errors
or omissions or for changes in the details given in this book or for
the consequences of any reliance on the information it provides. We
have tried to ensure accuracy in this book, but things do change and
we would be grateful if readers would advise us of any inaccuracies
they may encounter.

We have taken all reasonable steps to ensure that these walks are
safe and achievable by walkers with a realistic level of fitness.
However, all outdoor activities involve a degree of risk and the
publishers accept no responsibility for any injuries caused to
readers whilst following these walks. For more advice on walking
safely see page 128. The mileage range shown on the front cover
is for guidance only – some walks may exceed or be less than
these distances.

Visit the AA Publishing website at www.theAA.com

Paste-up and editorial by Outcrop Publishing Services Ltd, Cumbria
for AA Publishing

Colour reproduction by LC Repro
Printed in Italy by G Canale & C SPA, Torino, Italy

Legend

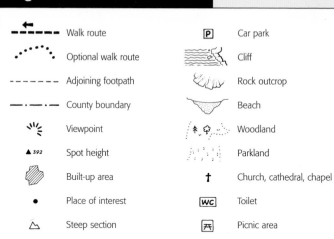

← ----	Walk route	P	Car park
••••••	Optional walk route	~~~	Cliff
-------	Adjoining footpath		Rock outcrop
—•—•—	County boundary		Beach
☀	Viewpoint	♣	Woodland
▲ 392	Spot height		Parkland
	Built-up area	†	Church, cathedral, chapel
•	Place of interest	WC	Toilet
△	Steep section	🛱	Picnic area

Berkshire & Buckinghamshire locator map

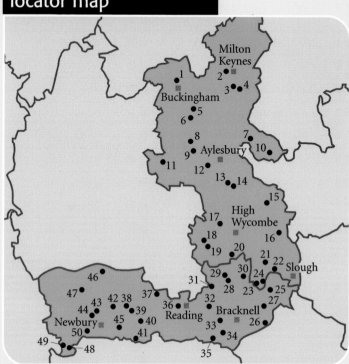

Contents

Contents

WALK	RATING	DISTANCE	PAGE

Rating: Each walk is rated for its relative difficulty compared to the other walks in this book. Walks marked 🚶🚶🚶 are likely to be shorter and easier with little total ascent. The hardest walks are marked 🚶🚶🚶 .

Walking in Safety: For advice and safety tips ➤ 128.

Introducing Berkshire & Buckinghamshire

The adjoining counties of Berkshire and Buckinghamshire have long been recognised as two of England's prettiest shires. Classically English in their beauty and character, they reflect the best of our countryside. Their delightful mix of beech woodland, rolling farmland, quiet waterways and breezy downland, conspiring to represent some of the finest walking country in Britain. As with many other counties, Berkshire and Buckinghamshire are blessed with many miles of public rights of way, and the routes chosen for this guide reach deep into their rural heartlands, taking advantage of a rich legacy of historic sites and fascinating landmarks.

Buckinghamshire is the larger of the two counties – its shape often compared to a lion rampant. This is a land of glorious beech trees, wide views and imposing country houses. The Victorian Prime Minister Benjamin Disraeli savoured the peace and tranquillity of Hughenden Manor, while generations of statesmen have entertained politicians and world leaders at Chequers, the Prime Minister's rural retreat. Stowe and Waddesdon Manor are fine examples of even grander houses, amid sumptuous gardens and dignified parkland.

The Vale of Aylesbury is a vast playground with 1,000 miles (1,609km) of paths and tracks to explore. Rising above it like protective guardians are the Chiltern Hills, a designated Area of Outstanding Natural Beauty covering 308sq miles (880sq km). They are best appreciated in autumn when the leaves of the beech trees turn from dark green to deep brown. In the south east corner of the Chilterns lie the woodland rides of Burnham Beeches, another haven for ramblers, wildlife lovers and those seeking peaceful recreation away from the noise and bustle of the city.

Buckinghamshire's history is long and eventful, but the county is also associated with events within living memory. At Bletchley Park, 60 years ago, more than 10,000 people worked in complete secrecy to try and bring a swift conclusion to the Second World War. Further south, an otherwise unremarkable stretch of railway line was made infamous by the Great Train Robbery in the summer of 1963.

Berkshire, too, has much to attract the walker. The county essentially consists of two distinct parts. The western half is predominantly rural, with the Lambourn Downs spilling down to

---

PUBLIC TRANSPORT ⓘ

Berkshire and Buckinghamshire are well served by public transport, making many of the walks in this guide easily accessible. For information about local bus services contact the Traveline on 0870 608 2608. Walks 2, 3, 15, 20, 25, 30, 31, 33, 36, 37 and 45 start at or near a railway station. For times of trains throughout the country call the 24 hour national train inquiry line on 08457 48 49 50. For countrywide public transport information look at the internet site www.pti.org.uk.

the River Lambourn and the Berkshire Downs to the more majestic Thames. The eastern half of Berkshire may be more urban but here, too, there is the opportunity to get out and savour open spaces. Windsor Great Park and Maidenhead Thicket are prime examples.

Threading their way through the county are two of the south's prettiest rivers – the Lambourn and the Pang. Beyond the tranquil tow paths of the Kennet and Avon Canal, Greenham Common's famous airbase has been transformed to delight walkers.

Towns and cities are a feature of this book, too. The sleepy backwaters of Reading provide a fascinating insight into how the town developed, while a tour of Milton Keynes demonstrates a bold step in city planning.

Each route offers a specific theme to enhance the walk, as well as snippets of useful information on what to look for and what to do while you're there. Most are circular, though some require a train to return to the start. Enjoy the walks and savour the delights of Berkshire and Buckinghamshire's countryside.

Using this Book

Information panels
An information panel for each walk shows its relative difficulty (➤ 5), the distance and total amount of ascent. An indication of the gradients you will encounter is shown by the rating ▲▲▲ (no steep slopes) to ▲▲▲ (several very steep slopes).

Maps
There are 30 maps, covering 40 of the walks. Some walks have a suggested option in the same area. The information panel for these walks will tell you how much extra walking is involved. On short-cut suggestions the panel will tell you the total distance if you set out from the start of the main walk. Where an option returns to the same point on the main walk, just the distance of the loop is given. Where an option leaves the main walk at one point and returns to it at another, then the distance shown is for the whole walk. The minimum time suggested is for reasonably fit walkers and doesn't allow for stops. Each walk has a suggested map. Laminated aqua3 maps are longer lasting and water resistant.

Start Points
The start of each walk is given as a six-figure grid reference prefixed by two letters indicating which 100km square of the National Grid it refers to. You'll find more information on grid references on most Ordnance Survey maps.

Dogs
We have tried to give dog owners useful advice about how dog friendly each walk is. Please respect other countryside users. Keep your dog under control, especially around livestock, and obey local bylaws and other dog control notices.

Car Parking
Many of the car parks suggested are public, but occasionally you may find you have to park on the roadside or in a lay-by. Please be considerate when you leave your car, ensuring that access roads or gates are not blocked and that other vehicles can pass safely.

Walk 1

Stowe's Fair, Majestic Paradise

Savour the delights of Stowe, with its famous 18th-century landscape garden and surrounding parkland.

•DISTANCE•	4½ miles (7.2km)
•MINIMUM TIME•	2hrs
•ASCENT / GRADIENT•	Negligible
•LEVEL OF DIFFICULTY•	
•PATHS•	Field paths, estate drives, stretches of road, 5 stiles
•LANDSCAPE•	Farmland and parkland
•SUGGESTED MAP•	aqua3 OS Explorer 192 Buckingham & Milton Keynes
•START / FINISH•	Grid reference: SP 684357
•DOG FRIENDLINESS•	Under control across farmland, on lead within Stowe Park
•PARKING•	On-street parking in Chackmore
•PUBLIC TOILETS•	Stowe Landscape Garden

BACKGROUND TO THE WALK

Stowe has been described as England's greatest work of art and possibly the world's most bewitching landscape garden. But how did it all begin? It was Sir Richard Temple (1634–97), one of Marlborough's generals and described as 'the greatest Whig in the army', who first built a brick mansion here. Work eventually came to an end in 1839 when Stowe's then owner, the 2nd Duke of Buckingham, a descendant of Lord Cobham, suffered financial problems and was declared bankrupt.

Temple's son (1669–1749, also Sir Richard) married a wealthy brewery heiress, became Lord, and later Viscount Cobham and began to extend the house and park. He prided himself on his reputation as a great radical – anti-Stuart and pro-liberty, greatly endorsing the ideals of the Glorious Revolution. Although work on the gardens at Stowe started in 1711, it wasn't until Lord Cobham fell out with the George II and his Prime Minister, Robert Walpole, that the idea of an experiment in 'moral gardening' really seized him.

Cobham threw himself wholeheartedly into the project. His aim was to create a garden of ideas; a place symbolising the notion of liberty. Historians maintain that Cobham was attempting to rewrite the history of Britain, using buildings and landscape.

Many Hands

In 1713 Stowe employed only half a dozen garden staff, but five years later there were almost 30 gardeners. Work at Stowe became a way of life, and so anxious was Cobham for the momentum not to be broken that, when his head gardener Edward Bissell broke his leg, he called for a specially adapted chair so that Bissell could continue to work.

In total, Cobham designed eight lakes, constructed more than three dozen temples, and commissioned 50 statues and 40 busts. The country's finest artists and designers, including James Gibbs, William Kent and Sir John Vanbrugh, were employed to help create what James Thomson described as 'the fair majestic paradise of Stowe'. Even Lancelot 'Capability' Brown had a hand in it, beginning his career here in 1741.

Lord Cobham's successors consolidated his work by improving and adding to the garden. However, by the mid-19th century, the family fortunes had ebbed away and the estate was sold. After a further sale in 1921, Cobham's vision of an earthly paradise, described by Alexander Pope as 'a work to wonder at', was left virtually empty. The house became a school and the National Trust acquired the garden in 1989.

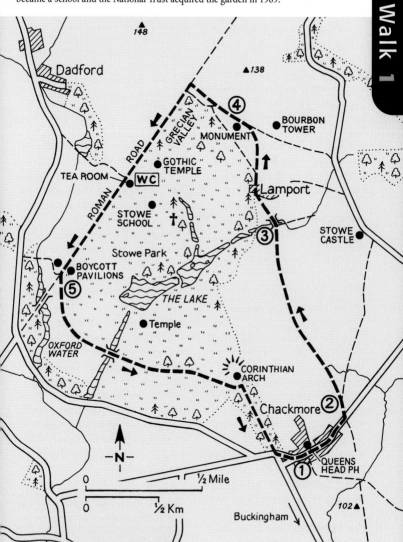

Walk 1 Directions

① Walk through **Chackmore**, pass the **Queens Head**, and continue through the village. At the speed derestriction signs, keep ahead for a few paces and look for a path on the left. Aim diagonally right in the field, passing under power lines. Make for a stile beneath the branches of an oak tree in the corner where waymarks indicate that the path forks.

Walk 1

② Cross the field towards two stiles, making for the one on the left, beyond which is a plank bridge. Keep to the right boundary of an elongated field and when it widens, go diagonally right to the far corner. **Stowe Castle** is over to the right, and to the left the outline of the **Corinthian Arch** is just visible among the trees. Join a track, pass under telegraph wires and look for a gap and waymark as the track curves right by the hedge corner. Veer over to the right in the field and look for a path signposted '**Farey Oak**'. Avoid this route and make for a footbridge and stile just a few paces away.

> **WHAT TO LOOK FOR** ⓘ
> The triangular **Gothic Temple**, used by the Landmark Trust as a holiday let, can be seen from the walk, as can **Stowe Castle**, a remarkable eye-catcher built in the 18th century. Look out, too, for the **Bourbon Tower**, which was built in the 1740s as a gamekeeper's lodge in iron-rich Northamptonshire limestone and given an octagonal turret in 1845.

③ Cross into the field and head up the slope, keeping to the left of two distant houses. Head for a single-storey dwelling in the top corner and as you climb the slope, the outline of the **Gothic Temple** looms into view. Go through a galvanised gate at **Lamport** and continue ahead on the bridleway. The **Bourbon Tower** is clearly visible over to the right. Pass through a gate and keep ahead towards a monument commemorating the Duke of Buckingham. Merge with another path and keep a sports ground on your right.

④ Make for a gate leading out to an avenue of trees running down towards the **Grecian Valley**. Cross

> **WHILE YOU'RE THERE** ⓘ
> The walk skirts the garden, offering good views of its classical features. Stowe is very large and visitors often allow most of the day for a leisurely tour. One of Stowe's most popular features is the **Grecian Valley**, overlooked by the Temple of Concorde and Victory. The valley was 'Capability' Brown's first large-scale design and consists of a lovely sloping glade with vistas towards monuments of Lord Cobham and General Wolfe.

over and follow the grass track up to a clump of trees. Bear left here and follow the wide avenue, part of a Roman road. Pass the magnificent façade of **Stowe School** and keep along the main drive. On reaching the **Boycott Pavilions**, branch off half left at a stile and sign for the Corinthian Arch. Down below lies the **Oxford Water**, crossed by a splendid 18th-century stone bridge.

⑤ Follow the drive through the parkland with glimpses of temples and classical designs. The drive eventually reaches the **Corinthian Arch**. Line up with the arch and pause here to absorb the breathtaking view of **Stowe School**, surely one of Britain's stateliest vistas. Walk down the avenue to the road junction, swing left and return to **Chackmore**.

> **WHERE TO EAT AND DRINK** ⓘ
> The **Queens Head** in Chackmore offers a range of traditional beers, including Banks. There is also a beer garden and a choice of meals and snacks – ranging from baguettes and chilli to lasagne and steak and kidney pudding. There is a licensed tea room at **Stowe**, serving morning coffee, light lunches and afternoon tea. A children's menu is also available. Alternatively, bring a picnic – permitted only in the Grecian Valley.

A Tour of Milton Keynes, City of the Future

See how a brand-new city has been shaped and styled on this unique walk with a strong architectural theme.

•DISTANCE•	3 miles (4.8km)
•MINIMUM TIME•	2hrs
•ASCENT / GRADIENT•	Negligble
•LEVEL OF DIFFICULTY•	
•PATHS•	Paved walkways, boulevards and park paths
•LANDSCAPE•	City centre and park
•SUGGESTED MAP•	aqua3 OS Explorer 192 Milton Keynes & Buckingham, or street map from tourist information centre
•START / FINISH•	Grid reference: SP 842380
•DOG FRIENDLINESS•	Probably not most dogs' idea of fun
•PARKING•	Car park at Milton Keynes Station
•PUBLIC TOILETS•	Milton Keynes Station and shopping centres

BACKGROUND TO THE WALK

Much has happened to Milton Keynes since 1967 when an area of almost 22,000 acres (8,910ha) was designated for the construction of a new city. But why Milton Keynes? The planners and architects of the day considered its location at the heart of England to be just about perfect. Centrally positioned within the country, only an hour from London by car on the new M1 motorway and easily accessible by train, the city's communication links were seen as ideal.

The First Settlers

It was in around 2000 BC that people first settled here and the remains of the earliest known house in the area date back to the late Bronze Age or early Iron Age. Later, the Romans occupied this part of the country, their farms and rural settlements were served by two towns – Lactodorum and Magiovinium. Near by ran Watling Street, now the A5, linking London, the West Midlands and North Wales.

During the 19th century the Milton Keynes area of Buckinghamshire began to expand, largely due to the dawning of the railway era that brought industrial prosperity to places like Newport Pagnell and Wolverton. The opening of the M1 in 1959 sealed the area's future as the site of a new city required to meet the demands of the business world and its employees, and accommodating a quarter of a million people within its boundaries. The task of housing a growing population became a priority and, as the 20th century drew to a close, attention was focused on Milton Keynes as *the* place to live and work.

The Birth of a New City

Richard Crossman, Minister of Housing and Local Government (1964–66) supported the plan for a new city. Initially it was envisaged that Milton Keynes would consist of high-density settlements connected by monorail to a commercial centre – an innovative move and a far cry from the old concept of garden suburbs as developed by the London planners. However, the monorail system was eventually shelved in favour of a dispersed network of housing within a grid pattern of roads.

With its tree-lined boulevards, green squares and stylish office buildings, it's hard not to be impressed by Milton Keynes. It may get a bad press in some quarters, and there are those who feel it has too strong an American influence, but the city has been designed with convenience, mobility and modern living in mind. There are many who say it works.

Walk 2 Directions

① With your back to the station, aim slightly left, line up with a row of flag-poles and make for two underpasses. Keep ahead along **Midsummer Boulevard**, passing the sculpture on the left. Make for the next subway and cross **Witan Gate** and **Upper 5th Street**. Swing

left just before the next subway to visit the domed **Church of Christ the Cornerstone**. Keep the church on your left and continue to **Silbury Boulevard**, passing under the subway.

② Turn right and pass **Milton Keynes Library and Exhibition Gallery**. Pass **North 9th Street** and a statue of the Lloyds black horse at

Lloyds Court. Swing right and pass under the road to approach the shopping centre at **Deer Walk**. Don't enter the complex here, but instead turn left and walk along to the next entrance at **Eagle Walk**. Go straight through, pass a map of the shopping centre and emerge at **Midsummer Boulevard**.

③ Turn left to **Field Walk** and turn right here to cross the boulevard. Bear left to reach the tourist information centre, **Milton Keynes Theatre** and the city's gallery. Continue ahead under the subway and cross the footbridge into **Campbell Park**. Skirt the round pond and make for the beacon that represents the highest point in the park. As you approach it, turn sharp right and follow the path as it snakes down through the park. Roughly 30yds (27m) before a

circular seat bear sharp right to join a grassy path alongside a fence. Make for a kissing gate and turn right. Walk along to the next path junction, with a kissing gate on the right. Turn left here, back towards the centre of Milton Keynes. Keep to the left to join a wide concrete ride and follow the waymarked city centre route.

④ Cross the road bridge to **Bankfield roundabout** and go straight ahead along **Avebury Boulevard**. Cross **Secklow Gate** and **Lower 10th Street**, and turn right into **Lower 9th Street**. Pass **The Point** and bear left into **Midsummer Place** shopping centre. Cross the concourse and pass the police station. The **Church of Christ the Cornerstone** can be seen from here. Keep left and return to **Avebury Boulevard**, turning right to the underpass. Walk down to **Grafton Gate**, veer right just before it and head for **Midsummer Boulevard**. Go through the underpasses and return to the railway station at the start.

Secrets of Bletchley Park

Puzzle over the enigma of Station X on this urban walk around Bletchley.

•DISTANCE•	5 miles (8km)
•MINIMUM TIME•	1hr 45min
•ASCENT / GRADIENT•	Negligble
•LEVEL OF DIFFICULTY•	
•PATHS•	Roads, park and field paths, canal tow path and riverside walk, 2 stiles
•LANDSCAPE•	Mixture of suburban streets and farmland
•SUGGESTED MAP•	aqua3 OS Explorer 192 Buckingham & Milton Keynes
•START / FINISH•	Grid reference: SP 868337
•DOG FRIENDLINESS•	Under control in Blue Lagoon Park, along Broad Walk and by canal. Dogs are permitted in grounds of Bletchley Park
•PARKING•	Bletchley Station and approach road
•PUBLIC TOILETS•	Bletchley Station and Bletchley Park

BACKGROUND TO THE WALK

Bletchley Park. The name may sound ordinary enough but what took place here during the dark days of the Second World War is quite remarkable. This was the home of Station X – where more than 10,000 people worked in total secrecy in a small, nondescript town at the heart of the English shires.

Brain Teasers

It was here that mathematicians, linguists, crossword enthusiasts and Oxbridge scholars battled for hours on end, in wooden huts and brick-built blocks, to break the seemingly unbreakable. Their role was to study the German military cipher machine, 'Enigma', and devise a programme to enable the Allies to decode the Nazis' secret radio messages, which often provided clues as to the enemy's next course of action. At times the code-breakers' task seemed impossible – after all, the odds against success were phenomenal. But they did succeed, shortening the war against Germany by as much as two years.

One of the key figures in the story of Bletchley Park was Alan Turing, a mathematical genius considered to be one of the pioneering fathers of the modern computer. It was he who invented the 'Bombe', an electro-mechanical machine of clattering code wheels intended to significantly reduce the time needed to break the daily-changing Enigma keys.

But why Bletchley Park? What was it about this Victorian mansion, built by a city financier, that made the men from British Intelligence choose it as their top secret Station X? Midway between the universities of Oxford and Cambridge and just a few minutes' walk from a mainline railway station with regular services to London and many other parts of the country, it seemed a perfect venue for the Government Code and Cypher School, which until then had been based at the Foreign Office. As the threat of war loomed, Bletchley Park was poised to become the key communications centre in the history of modern warfare.

In August 1939, code breakers arrived at Bletchley Park in large numbers. Their work had begun. They posed as members of 'Captain Ridley's shooting party' so as not to arouse suspicion in the area. Ridley was the man in charge of the school's move to Bletchley. For the next 40 years, no one outside Bletchley Park knew exactly what went on here, and so impeccable was the code breakers' professionalism that the Germans never even realised Enigma had been broken. Churchill called the staff at Bletchley Park his 'geese that laid the golden eggs but never cackled'.

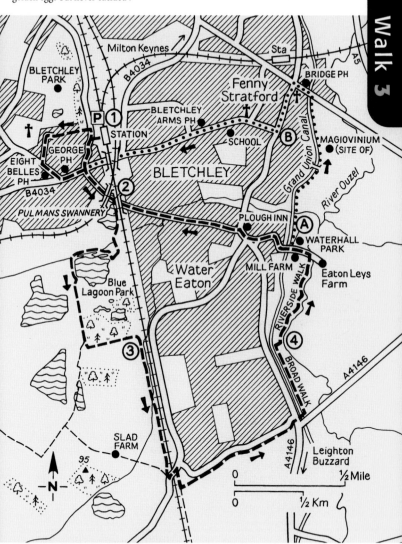

Walk 3 Directions

① From the station car park cross the road and take the path to **Bletchley Park**. On leaving the former Station X walk along **Wilton Avenue** and left into **Church Green Road**. Bear left at the junction with **Buckingham Road** and make your way towards Central Bletchley. Turn right into **Water Eaton Road**, pass beneath the Bletchley-to-Oxford railway line, and bear right at the footpath sign, just before the next railway bridge.

② Pass a pond, **Pulmans Swannery**, on the right and follow the fenced path to a stile. Continue to a fork, keep right and follow a track in an anti-clockwise direction round the edge of the lake. Avoid a ford and a footbridge and continue on the lakeside path. At the south west corner of the lake, look for some steps and a footbridge on the right. Turn left immediately beyond them and follow a path parallel to power lines. Bear left at a grassy track and follow it towards the railway line. Turn right immediately before a stile and keep to the right of a house. Swing left at a fence to reach a stile, and then walk ahead with the railway line on your left.

WHAT TO LOOK FOR ℹ️

The **Grand Union Canal** is perfect for exploring on foot. The tow path provides excellent views of this historic waterway, originally known as the Grand Junction Canal. Its construction took place between 1793 and 1800, resulting in many changes to the landscape, but, more importantly, it provided work and business opportunities for local people.

---

③ Pass through a tunnel of trees and alongside farmland and, when you reach the drive to **Slad Farm**, exit to the road. Bear left, cross the railway bridge and turn immediately right at a gate. Follow the path for a short distance to a field corner and swing left to join a bridleway. Keep the houses of

---

WHERE TO EAT AND DRINK ℹ️

The **Plough Inn**, on the closing stages of the walk, is handy for a pint, a hot meal or a snack. Near the start are the **Eight Belles** and the **George**, offering all-day breakfasts, jacket potatoes, toasties, fresh baguettes, lasagne and scampi. There are picnic tables between the river and the canal and at Waterhall Park.

Bletchley on your left, beyond the trees and hedgerow. On reaching the road, between two roundabouts, cross over to the canal bridge and swing left to follow the **Broad Walk**. At a sign for the **Riverside Walk**, turn right and then swing left after about 75yds (69m).

④ Keep the river a short distance away to the right. Draw level with a farm over to the right, cross a footbridge over a pond and turn left. Head for **The Watermill** and **Mill Farm**, avoiding the car park for **Waterhall Park**. Cross the bridge over the **Grand Union Canal** and keep right. Ahead now are several thatched and timber-framed cottages. Turn left in front of them and keep right at the main road junction, heading towards the **Plough** inn. Cross the road at the roundabout, following the sign for the station. Continue ahead through a residential area, pass beneath the two railway bridges seen near the start of the walk, go straight over at the junction and back to the station car park.

WHILE YOU'RE THERE ℹ️

After the war the intelligence services continued to use part of the park as a training centre and the site was also used as a training college for teachers, post office workers and air traffic controllers. It was decommissioned in 1987 and in 1992 the **Bletchley Park Trust** was born to preserve the historic site. There's lots to see here so allow plenty of time for your visit. Props from the film *Enigma* (2001) are on display, the museum illustrates many Second World War activities and you can follow the Cryptology Trail, learning how messages were intercepted and delivered to Bletchley Park. Also on display is a replica of Colossus, the world's first programmable electronic computer.

On to Magiovinium

A longer variation on Walk 3, passes the site of a Roman town.
See map and information panel for Walk 3

•DISTANCE•	6½ miles (10.4km)
•MINIMUM TIME•	2hr 45min
•ASCENT / GRADIENT•	Negligble
•LEVEL OF DIFFICULTY•	🚶🚶 🚶 🚶

Walk 4 Directions (Walk 3 option)

At Point Ⓐ, with **Waterhall Park** on your right, join the tow path of the **Grand Union Canal** and follow it north towards **Fenny Stratford**. Pass a milepost 'Braunston 39 miles'. Head for the bridge and keep ahead, with the tower of **Fenny Stratford church** in view among the rooftops on the opposite bank.

The land over to the right was once part of the Roman town of Magiovinium. The bank and ditch surrounding it can be identified in aerial photographs and the site is protected as a scheduled ancient monument. The enclosed part of Magiovinium straddles Watling Street and covered about 18½ acres (7.5ha). The interior layout of the town, which was unwalled, would have comprised a grid pattern of streets along similar lines to neighbouring Milton Keynes.

Head towards a suspension bridge and a private marina. Leave the tow path just beyond it, turn left at the road and pass the **Bridge** pub, the **Roman Way Tavern** and the **Swan**. Bear left into **Aylesbury Street**, signposted 'Central Bletchley and

Water Eaton'. Pass the church on the corner and walk along to the **Maltsters Arms** and the **Bull and Butcher** inn. Continue to the mini-roundabout and turn right into **Vicarage Road**, Point Ⓑ.

Bletchley and Fenny Stratford are like period pieces and many of the Victorian and Edwardian houses in these streets have changed little since the Second World War when large numbers of the code breakers working at nearby Bletchley Park were billeted here. Most spare rooms were let at that time.

Pass **Browne Willis Close** and **Queensway Methodist church** and follow the road to **Knowles Middle School**, built in 1937. Adjacent to it is **Knowles Nursery School**. Further down on the right is the **Bletchley Arms**. Follow a pedestriansed street and keep ahead at the next road, between shops. Pass the **Conservative Club** on the right and, when the road bends right, go forward towards the Brunel shopping centre. Follow the sign for the railway station and **Bletchley Park**, go straight ahead at the roundabout and pass the **Park** pub on the left. Pass beneath the railway line, turn right at the police station into **Sherwood Drive** and return to the station.

Walk 5

Trailing Around Addington

Follow field paths to the heart of the countryside, part of a unique network of rights of way throughout England and Wales.

•DISTANCE•	4¼ miles (6.8km)
•MINIMUM TIME•	1hr 45min
•ASCENT / GRADIENT•	88ft (27m) ▲ ▲ ▲
•LEVEL OF DIFFICULTY•	🚶 🚶 🚶
•PATHS•	Quiet country road, stretches of field paths, North Buckinghamshire Way and Cross Bucks Way, 13 stiles
•LANDSCAPE•	Gently undulating farmland either side of Claydon Brook
•SUGGESTED MAP•	aqua3 OS Explorer 192 Buckingham & Milton Keynes
•START / FINISH•	Grid reference: SP 742285
•DOG FRIENDLINESS•	On lead on road and near livestock
•PARKING•	Limited space by church in Addington
•PUBLIC TOILETS•	None on route

Walk 5 Directions

In recent years the simple activity of walking has become one of Britain's most popular outdoor pastimes, With 140,000 miles (225,260km) of rights of way in England and Wales alone, it's hardly surprising that people spend so much of their leisure time eagerly exploring the hills and dales, woods and moorland to be found in this glorious countryside.

Some footpaths came into being as vital trade routes or packhorse trails, while others were drove roads established to convey sheep and cattle. Pilgrim tracks and green lanes steered medieval wayfarers between the great centres of Christianity, Winchester and Canterbury. In the 18th and 19th centuries the agricultural revolution and Enclosure Acts were responsible for major changes in the countryside, producing a vastly different, almost unrecognisable landscape and introducing a host of new paths and tracks.

Over recent years many long distance trails have appeared on Britain's rights of way map. These range from 10 miles (16.2km) to over 300 miles (486km) and reflect the best of our varied countryside and ever-changing scenery. Two of Buckinghamshire's more popular trails meet on this walk, providing ramblers with the opportunity to explore the rural heart of the county. The Cross Bucks Way runs across Buckinghamshire for

---

WHILE YOU'RE THERE

Addington's secluded **church** stands at the end of a long drive and is renowned for its windows, which contain the largest collection of Netherlandish glass in England. The roundels are 16th and early 17th century and the windows mainly illustrate biblical scenes. Sir Malcolm Sargeant (1895–1967), the famous conductor, lived in a cottage at Addington during the Second World War and sometimes played the church organ.

WHAT TO LOOK FOR

At **Verney Junction** you can see the remains of the old station, which was in use when trains ran along this line between Oxford and Bletchley. It is some years since the railway here was in regular use, though there are plans to integrate it into a long distance east to west rail route. Curiously, this remote station once represented the end of the Metropolitan Line, over 50 miles (80km) from Baker Street in London.

---

24 miles (39km) from the Oxfordshire border to the Grand Union Canal near Leighton Buzzard, while the North Buckinghamshire Way is 30 miles (48km) long and extends from Chequers to Milton Keynes.

Keep **Addington Church** on your right and an executive house with a well in the front garden on your left and follow the **North Bucks Way** out of Addington, across farmland. Make for a stile and footbridge over the **Claydon Brook**. Continue ahead to a stile and plank bridge and keep to the right edge of the next field. Over to the left lies **Furzen Farm**. Cross a track and make for a kissing gate leading out to a disused railway. The old 'stop, look and listen' sign is still in place – requesting drivers to 'notify the local British Rail manager before crossing with a vehicle which is unusually long, wide, low, heavy or slow-moving'. Follow the **North Bucks Way**, keeping the old 1870 station buildings on the right.

The canopied entrance is a reminder of the days when **Verney Junction** was a working station. Look out, too, for the Victorian post box. Walk along the road to the **Verney Arms Country Bistro** and keep right at the junction. Follow

the road to **Littleworth Farm** and bear right at the next junction for Buckingham and Padbury. Re-cross the old railway at the next bridge and continue along the road, following it round a left bend. Turn right just before **Claydon Hill Farm** and join the **Cross Bucks Way**. Cross a stile and bridge and follow the fence along to a second stile.

Go diagonally right in the next field, passing under electricity cables, and cross a dismantled railway via two stiles. Go straight ahead in the next field to a galvanised gate and then veer to the left of a stand of trees. Look for a stile and footbridge and veer diagonally right. Across the field are two gates; make for the left-hand one and head diagonally up the field, towards the top right corner. Draw level with **Hill Farm**, pass through a gate and maintain the same direction to reach a track and two stiles. Aim diagonally right across the field to a stile and galvanised gate and go straight ahead in the next field to a stile, footbridge and waymark. Don't cross over, but perform a 150 degree turn and head for two stiles in the boundary hedge.

Head diagonally right towards the houses of **Addington** and make for a stile by a lane. Bear left by the telephone box and walk along to a road junction with a traffic arrow. Turn right here, then bear right again at the next junction and return to the **church**.

WHERE TO EAT AND DRINK

The **Verney Arms Country Bistro** at Verney Junction welcomes walkers and offers an imaginative menu. Typical lunch dishes include pie of the day, steak sandwich and shepherds pie.

Claydon's Lady with the Lamp

Walk 6

Visit a splendid National Trust house and see the bedroom occupied by Florence Nightingale on this country walk around the Claydon villages.

•DISTANCE•	5½ miles (8.8km)
•MINIMUM TIME•	2hrs
•ASCENT / GRADIENT•	160ft (49m) ▲ ▲ ▲
•LEVEL OF DIFFICULTY•	🚶🚶 🚶🚶 🚶🚶
•PATHS•	Field paths and tracks, several stretches of road
•LANDSCAPE•	Gentle farmland and parkland in the Vale of Aylesbury
•SUGGESTED MAP•	aqua3 OS Explorer 192 Buckingham & Milton Keynes
•START / FINISH•	Grid reference: SP 739255
•DOG FRIENDLINESS•	Dogs on lead at all times, some fields with livestock
•PARKING•	On-street parking in road leading to St Mary the Virgin Church, East Claydon
•PUBLIC TOILETS•	Claydon House

BACKGROUND TO THE WALK

Standing amid elegant parkland, studded with cedar and cypress trees, is 18th-century Claydon House, replacing a much earlier building and now in the care of the National Trust. Only one third of the house remains and, seeing it for the first time, you may be struck by its simplicity, yet it presents to the visitor a series of magnificent and highly distinctive rococo state rooms with carving by Luke Lightfoot, said to be his only known work. Also on view is the bedroom used by Florence Nightingale (1820–1910) during her visits to her sister who lived here.

Claydon House

In 1620 Edmund Verney, Knight-Marshal and Standard Bearer to Charles I, became the first Verney to occupy Claydon. Later, during the 18th century, the family succeeded to an earldom and Edmund's great great grandson, Ralph, 2nd Earl Verney, began to remodel the Tudor manor house, attempting to outdo nearby Stowe (► Walk 1). This work still forms the core of the three-storey brick east wing, although the design has disappeared as a result of successive rebuilding. Ralph also added the stone-faced west wing, employing the services of the unknown Luke Lightfoot, an eccentric and enigmatic figure who had acquired certain skills as a craftsman and was variously described as a cabinetmaker, carver, architect and surveyor.

Penniless and Miserable

However, there was a darker side to Lightfoot. He was also a swindler, which almost certainly came to light just as his work was nearing completion, as he was dismissed in 1769. Undeterred, Verney continued with his building plan, though now beset by financial problems. He added a domed entrance hall to the west wing and beyond that a ballroom, but died soon after in 1791, penniless and miserable. His niece, Lady Fermanagh, inherited

Claydon and within a year she had demolished her uncle's precious ballroom and entrance hall. The house was bequeathed by the Verney family to the National Trust in 1956.

The Lady With the Lamp

Florence Nightingale, whose sister married Sir Harry Verney, was a frequent visitor to Claydon between the late 1850s and 1895. She would often spend her summers at the house and over the fireplace in her bedroom is a portrait of the *Lady with the Lamp* by W B Richmond. Adjacent to it is a watercolour by Chalon depicting Florence, her sister and their mother. A museum displays Verney family mementoes and objects associated with Florenence Nightingale and her experiences during the Crimean War.

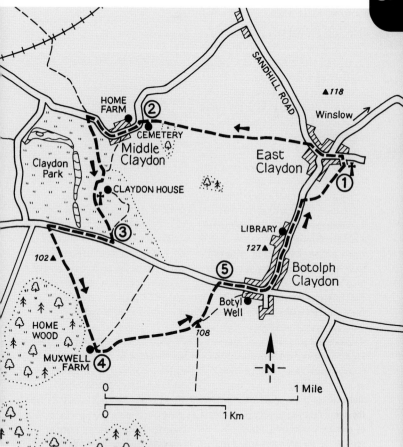

Walk 6 Directions

① Walk along **Church Way** and continue ahead in the village centre. Keep right at the next junction, following **Sandhill Road**. Pass a row of houses set back from the road

and swing left just before a brick and timber cottage to pass through a galvanised gate. Go straight ahead towards the next gate and look for a gate and waymark a few paces to the left of it. Keep ahead in the field, with the boundary on your right. Make for a gate in the corner

WHILE YOU'RE THERE

If time allows, leave the route of the walk near Claydon House and explore the local countryside on permissive paths. The routes are part of what is known as the **Conservation Walks Project**, which is funded by companies under the Landfill Tax Credit Scheme. Open permitted access allows walkers to enjoy Claydon's parkland and walk round the lakes to the west of the house.

and cross the field to the boundary. Continue ahead with the hedgerow on the left and follow a track along the field perimeter, heading for the buildings of **Home Farm**. Look for a plank bridge and stile to the left of the track and cross the cemetery to a stile by the road.

② Bear left and follow the road for 600yds (549m), passing the entrance to **Home Farm** on the right and a footpath on the left. Turn left and follow the drive to **Claydon House** and when you reach a cattle grid just in front of it, bear right through two gates and turn left. Keep Claydon House and the church on your left and continue alongside the ha-ha, with the lake over to your right. Cut through the parkland to a gate, merge with the drive to **Claydon House** and follow it to the road.

③ Turn right and pass a lay-by. Continue along the roadside until you reach a stile in the left boundary. Head diagonally left towards a hedge corner and make for a stile close to it. Maintain the same direction, make for the extreme left corner of **Home Wood**, cross a second stile and look for a third stile by the woodland edge, leading into the next field. Keep telegraph wires on your left and look for a waymark in the corner. Cross a stile and keep to the left of a hedge. Make for a gate and stile ahead and cross a tarmac drive to **Muxwell Farm**.

WHERE TO EAT AND DRINK

There are no pubs on the route of the walk. However, nearby **Winslow** and **Buckingham** offer a good choice of inns, cafés and restaurants. Refreshments are also available at **Claydon House**.

④ Beyond a gate, head diagonally left and look for a waymark in the line of trees across the pasture. Veer right in the next field, making for a stile and post in the boundary. Walk diagonally right across the field to the far corner, pass through a gap and keep to the right edge of the pasture. Bear right at a gateway to a track and turn left. Walk along to the road and turn right.

⑤ Walk through **Botolph Claydon** and bear left at the junction, following the signs for East Claydon and Winslow. Pass **Botolph Farmhouse** and the village **library** and hall. Follow the pavement to a sign 'footpath only, no horses'. Take the path back to **East Claydon**.

WHAT TO LOOK FOR

St Mary the Virgin Church at East Claydon is tucked away on the edge of the village. Its record of presiding rectors dates back to 1218. The tower was built in the late 15th century, while the chapel was added to the nave in 1230. Over the years the local villages have united to become the parish of the Claydons. Look out for the former **library** at Botolph Claydon, built in 1900 and now the village hall. Adjacent to it is a clock tower erected in 1913 by the friends and parishioners of Sir Edmund Verney in remembrance of his work for the welfare of the parish and his gift of the hall and library.

Mentmore and the Crime of the Century

A pleasant amble in the Vale of Aylesbury, passing the site of the 20th century's most audacious crime.

•DISTANCE•	6½ miles (10.4km)
•MINIMUM TIME•	2hrs 45min
•ASCENT / GRADIENT•	180ft (55m) ▲▲▲
•LEVEL OF DIFFICULTY•	🚶🚶 🚶🚶 🚶🚶
•PATHS•	Field paths and tracks, roads and canal tow path, 2 stiles
•LANDSCAPE•	Vale of Aylesbury and farmland west of Grand Union Canal
•SUGGESTED MAP•	aqua3 OS Explorers 181 Chiltern Hills North; 192 Milton Keynes & Buckingham
•START / FINISH•	Grid reference: SP 907196 (on Explorer 181)
•DOG FRIENDLINESS•	On lead across farmland and under control on tow path
•PARKING•	Limited parking in vicinity of Stag pub at Mentmore
•PUBLIC TOILETS•	None on route

BACKGROUND TO THE WALK

It hardly seems possible today, but in the summer of 1963, 15 masked men waited in the darkness of the Buckinghamshire countryside, held up the night train from Glasgow to London and robbed it of £2.5 million It was described as the crime of the century, making newspaper headlines around the world and eventually turning the robbers into folk heroes, immortalised in books, television series and money-spinning movies. The robbers were pursued and captured by Scotland Yard and many of them were given long prison sentences. But the story did not end there. One of them, Ronald Biggs, broke out of jail, fled to Brazil and eluded capture for the next 35 years.

These days, surplus and used bank notes are transported around the country in security vans, but in the very different world of the early 1960s, express trains conveyed such consignments – often with huge amounts of money on board. And 40 years ago it was possible to stop a mail train and rob it – as was proved.

The men planned the snatch in meticulous detail, surveying the railway line between London and Rugby in an attempt to find an isolated stretch of track with a signal and easy access to the road. Eventually they found what they were looking for – Sears Crossing and nearby Bridego Bridge on the Buckinghamshire/Bedfordshire border, to the south of Leighton Buzzard. They made many trips here in the dead of night, to identify the mail trains and plan the job.

Satisfied that it could be done, the next step was to familiarise themselves with the technicalities of train engines and braking systems. To do this, they dressed up in navy blue boiler suits, passing themselves off as railway workers in the marshalling yards of London's mainline stations. In the early hours of Thursday 8 August, 1963, the men were as ready as they ever would be. It was time to go.

Travelling in a convoy of vehicles, they made their way across country to the four-track railway. Their first task was to cut the telephone wires to the nearby farms. Then, as the mail train approached, they covered the green light with a glove and used a battery and a bulb behind the red signal to give the impression to the driver that the light was against him.

The train stopped, but the driver refused to co-operate and received violent blows to the head. With the engine and the vital post office coaches detached from the rest of the train, the men moved the express down the line to Bridego Bridge where they unloaded 120 sacks on to the vehicles lined up on the road below. They drove off as dawn gradually lit the scene of their extraordinary crime. (➤ Walk 11 to find out what happened next.)

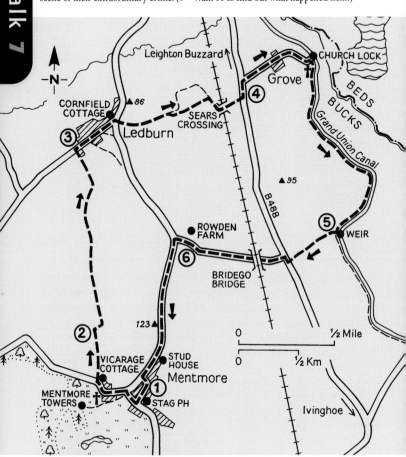

Walk 7 Directions

① Walk back to the junction by the **Stag**, turn right and pass one of the grand entrances to **Mentmore Towers**. Follow the road round to the left, then to the right by the **Church of St Mary the Virgin**. Continue along the road and bear right at a stile, just beyond **Vicarage Cottage**. Go down the field, keeping the fence over to the right, and look for a stile in the bottom boundary.

② Veer right for a few paces to a plank bridge, and then swing left to skirt the field, keeping a ditch on the right. On reaching the next plank bridge and waymark, look for a pond enclosed by fencing. Follow the path alongside it into the next field and pass under telegraph wires to the next plank bridge in the boundary. Go straight ahead and pass under electricity cables. The houses of **Ledburn** can be seen ahead. Make for a footbridge and in the next field aim slightly left, towards a house. Keep to the left of it and turn right at the road.

③ Walk through **Ledburn** and make for a left bend. On the left is **Cornfield Cottage**, once a chapel. Cross the road to a galvanised kissing gate and follow a track running across farmland. As it curves left, go straight on, following the path across a field. On reaching a track, turn right and follow it to **Sears Crossing**. Cross the railway bridge, follow the track down to the road and turn left.

④ Bear right at the sign for Grove Church and Farm and walk down to the **Grand Union Canal** at **Church Lock**. Pass **Church Lock Cottage** before turning right to join the canal tow path. Follow the Grand Union for about 1 mile (1.6km) and, about 140yds (128m)

before a bridge, where you can see a weir on the left, leave the tow path at a plank bridge and bear right for a few paces to the field corner.

⑤ Swing left and keep the boundary on your right. Make for two galvanised gates leading out to the road, turn right and then left at the turning for **Wing** and **Ledburn**. Follow the road to **Bridego Bridge**, pass beneath the railway and keep ahead to **Rowden Farm**.

⑥ Bear left at the next junction for **Mentmore**. Pass **Mentmore Courts** and the **Stud House** before turning left at the end of a stretch of pavement. Opposite the junction are two wooden gates leading into a field. Follow the road round to the right and return to the playground and parking area.

Making Tracks at Quainton

Recall the great days of steam travel on this walk to Waddesdon.

Walk 8

•DISTANCE•	5 miles (8km)
•MINIMUM TIME•	2hrs
•ASCENT / GRADIENT•	Negligible
•LEVEL OF DIFFICULTY•	
•PATHS•	Mainly field paths, some stretches of road, parts of North Buckinghamshire Way and Midshires Way, 22 stiles
•LANDSCAPE•	Gentle farmland in Vale of Aylesbury
•SUGGESTED MAP•	aqua3 OS Explorer 181 Chiltern Hills North
•START / FINISH•	Grid reference: SP 736189
•DOG FRIENDLINESS•	Mostly on lead, particularly near farm buildings
•PARKING•	Brill Tramway Path car park, parking on extreme left. Permission given by Buckinghamshire Railway Centre
•PUBLIC TOILETS•	Buckinghamshire Railway Centre

BACKGROUND TO THE WALK

The Buckinghamshire Railway Centre is one of those wonderful visitor attractions where, if you've the spirit and the imagination, you can wallow for hours in nostalgia, reliving the days when Britain could be justly proud of its railway system.

Covering 25 acres (10ha), the site boasts one of the country's largest independent collections of railway engines and rolling stock, with vintage steam train rides and half-day steam locomotive driving courses among its attractions. As you begin your tour of the centre, gazing in awe at the Victorian station with its flower-filled platform and adverts for seaside holidays, and the steam engines, the leviathans of the railway age, being restored in the nearby sheds, spare a moment to consider how it all began.

In 1968 the London Railway Preservation Society decided on Quainton Road Station to store old railway stock and memorabilia, leading to the birth of a new railway visitor attraction. Significantly, it chose the meeting point of three railways – the Metropolitan Railway, the Brill Tramway and the London extension of the Great Central Railway. The London Railway Preservation Society became the Quainton Railway Society Ltd whose dedicated members now own and operate the Buckinghamshire Railway Centre.

Originally opened in 1868 as part of the Aylesbury and Buckingham Railway, Quainton Road Station was absorbed by the Metropolitan Railway in 1890, becoming one of those far-flung rural stations you tend to associate with the best of Ealing comedy films. In those days you could change at Quainton Road for the Metropolitan Line and travel all the way to Baker Street. Look out for the authentic station sign on the platform at Quainton Road, advising passengers to change here for the Metropolitan Line. By the turn of the 19th century, it was also possible to travel from here direct to London's Marylebone or north to Manchester.

However, the Beeching cuts of the 1960s finally sounded the line's death knell. In 1963 the station closed to passenger traffic and three years later the Great Central main line closed and the line through the station was reduced to a single track. Today, the line may be quieter but the crowds still fill the platforms, savouring the thrill of a ride on a steam train.

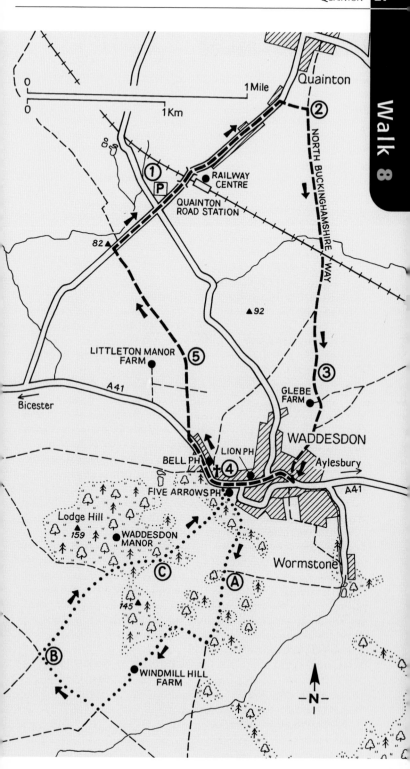

Walk 8

Walk 8 **Directions**

① Leave the car park, turn left and cross the road bridge over the railway. From the bridge there is a good view of the railway centre and the preserved station. The entrance to the site is on the right. On leaving the railway centre, bear right and follow **Station Road** towards **Quainton**. Pass lines of houses and, when the road curves round to the left by a bus stop, turn right at a footpath sign and stile to follow a track between fields. Quainton and its windmill can be seen over to the left. Go through a gateway and turn right to join the **North Buckinghamshire Way**.

WHERE TO EAT AND DRINK

There are refreshments at the **Buckinghamshire Railway Centre** and several pubs in nearby Waddesdon, including the **Lion**, which offers a daily menu, and the **Bell** where you may find chicken, ham and leek pie among a range of dishes. Morning coffee and afternoon tea are also served.

---

② Follow the edge of the field to a gate and continue to a stile in the distant boundary. Cross three more stiles before reaching the railway line, **Quainton Road Station** lies away to your right. Cross two stiles and follow a track to a right-hand bend. The outline of **Waddesdon Manor** can now be glimpsed up in the trees, to the right of the church. As the track bends right, cross a stile into the field and turn immediately right.

③ Skirt **Glebe Farm** and cross a track via two stiles, continuing on the **North Buckinghamshire Way**. Aim diagonally right to two stiles and continue alongside a hedgerow

in the next field. Cross two stiles and join an enclosed path running into **Waddesdon**. On reaching the **A41**, turn right, crossing **Quainton Road** and **Frederick Street**. Pass the **Lion**, the Methodist church and the post office before reaching the parish church of **St Michael and All Angels** on the right.

WHAT TO LOOK FOR

At 158ft (48m) long, including the tower, **St Michael and All Angels** at Waddesdon is a spacious church. It celebrated its 800th anniversary in 1990, the first stones of the church you see today were laid around 1190.

---

④ Follow the road out of the village, passing the **Bell** pub. Keep to the **A41** and look for an old stone milepost, 'London 44 miles'. In 50yds (46m), beyond the speed derestriction sign, turn right at a stile and waymark. Cut through the trees to a second stile and continue ahead in the field. Cross a concrete farm track, pass under power lines and aim for a stile in the boundary hedge. **Littleton Manor Farm** can be seen near by.

⑤ Aim slightly left in the next field to reach a stile and then go diagonally left across the next pasture to the far corner. Look for a narrow gap in the hedgerow, cross two stiles and walk ahead, passing alongside some corrugated animal shelters. Make for two stiles, turn right and follow the road back to the **car park**.

WHILE YOU'RE THERE

Make a point of looking at the **Buckinghamshire Railway Centre**'s superb new visitor centre, which opened in 2001 and is housed in a former Oxford station, painstakingly rebuilt at Quainton Road.

Waddesdon Five Arrows

An extra loop through parkland, glimpsing a sumptuous château.
See map and information panel for Walk 8

•DISTANCE•	3 miles (4.8km)
•MINIMUM TIME•	1hr 15min
•ASCENT / GRADIENT•	250ft (76m) ▲ ▲ ▲
•LEVEL OF DIFFICULTY•	🚶 🚶 🚶

Walk 9 Directions (Walk 8 option)

Mayer Amschel Rothschild founded the famous banking dynasty in Frankfurt in the 18th century. The family coat of arms focuses on a red shield and includes a fist holding five arrows. The arrows represent his five sons, four of whom left Frankfurt to establish banking houses in Europe's other financial centres – London, Vienna, Naples and Paris. Close family ties between the branches were maintained over the years, consolidated by intra-family marriages. Several of the houses in Waddesdon, including the village hall, were rebuilt by Ferdinand de Rothschild and can be distinguished by maroon gables and other architectural detail. Look out for the five arrows seen on various buildings during this walk.

Before Point ④ on Walk 8, just beyond the **Five Arrows** pub, turn left by the war memorial. Avoid the path on the right and head for the public entrance to **Waddesdon Manor**, a French Renaissance-style château built by Ferdinand de Rothschild in the late 19th century. Continue on the drive through the parkland. Follow it to a triangular junction, Point Ⓐ, keep right for a few paces and then veer left at the sign for **Windmill Hill Farm**. Continue on the bridleway as it bends right and left. At the farm buildings, follow the track left and then immediately right, passing a pair of cottages on the left. Descend the slope to a gate and turn right. Skirt the field, make for a ditch in the corner and continue ahead. Head for the next boundary, go through the gates and turn right at a stile, Point Ⓑ.

Walk ahead, keeping to the field boundary, and head for a stile. Continue along the field perimeter to a footbridge and two stiles on the right. Veer diagonally left in the adjacent field and head for a gap in the trees. Go up the slope to a broad drive, veer right and pass a waymark as you emerge from the woodland. Branch half left at the next waymark, Point Ⓒ, and take the grassy path across the slopes.

Head for a stile and follow the path, towards a curtain of woodland. Head for a gate, pick your way through the trees to a drive and cross over towards Waddesdon. Pass some garages and a house with the five arrows emblem before returning to the war memorial at Point ④ on Walk 8.

Walk 10

Topping Ivinghoe Beacon

Climb to a lofty viewpoint before following Britain's oldest road.

•DISTANCE•	4 miles (6.4km)
•MINIMUM TIME•	1hr 45min
•ASCENT / GRADIENT•	280ft (85m) ▲▲▲
•LEVEL OF DIFFICULTY•	👫 👫 👫
•PATHS•	Farmland and woodland paths, some road walking, 9 stiles
•LANDSCAPE•	Mix of remote farmland and typical Chiltern scenery
•SUGGESTED MAP•	aqua3 OS Explorer 181 Chiltern Hills North
•START / FINISH•	Grid reference: SP 963160
•DOG FRIENDLINESS•	On lead across initial farmland and under control on Icknield Way and Ridgeway
•PARKING•	Official car park near Ivinghoe Beacon
•PUBLIC TOILETS•	None on route

Walk 10 Directions

Ivinghoe Beacon is a suitably dramatic setting for the start of the Ridgeway. You can picture this ancient trade route as it once was, busy with travellers. Cattle drovers used it regularly, as did locals on short journeys, long distance traders and pilgrims.

Leave the car park for the road and keep left. Pass a track on the left and cross a cattle grid. Continue through woodland to a gate and footpath sign on the left. Skirt the field, keeping trees on the left, to a gate. Veer half left in the next field, keeping to the left of **Ward's Hurst Farm**. Cross a stile, look for a

> **WHERE TO EAT AND DRINK** ⓘ
> There are no pubs on the route of the walk, but many of the surrounding towns and villages offer a good choice of food and drink. Try the **Stag** at Mentmore (► Walk 7), the historic **Greyhound** coaching inn at Aldbury or one of the waterside pubs at Marsworth near Tring.

waymark by the outbuildings, bear left and keep the fence on your right. Pass under power lines to a stile and take the **Icknield Way** through the **Ashridge Estate**.

Follow the waymarked trail through woodland to a kissing gate and continue ahead, avoiding the Boundary Trail branching off to the right. Cross a stile and keep the fence on the left, climbing gently via two stiles to a marker stone for the **Icknield Way**, the **Peddars Way** and the **Ridgeway**. Turn right to a gate and stile and follow a clear track striking out across expansive downland. Head up the steep slope to the ridge and bear left to a stile. This stretch of the walk offers grand views of Ivinghoe Beacon and the surrounding countryside. Walk ahead at the Ridgeway sign, making for the start of the National Trail.

The Ridgeway extends for 85 miles (137km) through the Buckinghamshire Chilterns to the Thames and then across Berkshire into Wiltshire. In places the trail is as wide as a main road or a dual carriageway. When the original line became weathered or difficult to negotiate, travellers moved from one side to the other, gradually making the track wider.

The character of the Ridgeway changes the further west you travel. Initially, the trail cuts through gentle beech wood scenery, glorious in autumn, and across soft rolling hills where there are glimpses of distant horizons. Once across the Thames, the landscape assumes a totally different character. From the river onwards, the Ridgeway cuts across bleak, exposed downland, offering little in the way of shelter on a wet or windy day. This stretch of the Ridgeway explores a landscape littered with long barrows, prehistoric forts and monuments to the distant past.

> **WHILE YOU'RE THERE** ℹ
> The walk crosses the magnificent National Trust **Ashridge Estate**, which straddles the borders of Buckinghamshire and Hertfordshire, along the main ridge of the Chilterns. The estate includes a variety of woodlands, commons and chalk downland, with all manner of wildlife and plenty of superb scenery.

The downs of Berkshire and Wiltshire and the softer country of the Chilterns are remnants of a landscape of huge domes and ridges formed around 25 million years ago. The upper strata consists of great ridges of chalk laid down in the sea probably more than 60 million years ago.

Whether you are interested in history or geology, a walk along the Ridgeway is a journey through time. Here you can walk for miles without seeing another soul,

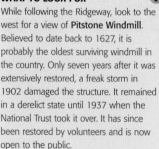

> **WHAT TO LOOK FOR** ℹ
> While following the Ridgeway, look to the west for a view of **Pitstone Windmill**. Believed to date back to 1627, it is probably the oldest surviving windmill in the country. Only seven years after it was extensively restored, a freak storm in 1902 damaged the structure. It remained in a derelict state until 1937 when the National Trust took it over. It has since been restored by volunteers and is now open to the public.

following in the footsteps of 300 generations and seeing the same tracts of chalk downland, the same distant hills and the same broad river. Today, walkers can follow the route from start to finish, but that hasn't always been the case. In 1942 the Ramblers Association proposed a long distance route across this part of southern England, but it was another 30 years before it was officially opened to the public. With its access to villages and overnight accommodation, many people choose the Ridgeway for a very pleasant walking holiday, allowing up to a week to complete the route at a leisurely pace.

With your back to the **Ridgeway plinth**, follow the trail as it runs south. Descend steeply, keep left at the fork and make for the road. Cross over and continue on the **National Trail**, beginning a moderate climb. Cut between trees before spotting a deep combe cutting in to the hillside on the right. Pass a gate and stile and when the Ridgeway sweeps right by a waymark, bear left and head up the steep slope to a stile. Cross a track just beyond it and follow the woodland footpath until you reach the drive to **Clipper Down Cottage**. Join the road here, turn left and return to the car park.

Walk 11

Brill and a Farmhouse Den of Thieves

Enjoy good views across Buckinghamshire on this breezy walk beginning in a sprawling hilltop village.

•DISTANCE•	4½ miles (7.2km)
•MINIMUM TIME•	1hr 30min
•ASCENT / GRADIENT•	350ft (107m) ▲▲▲
•LEVEL OF DIFFICULTY•	林 林 林
•PATHS•	Field paths and tracks, several stretches of road, 8 stiles
•LANDSCAPE•	Mixture of farmland and rolling country
•SUGGESTED MAP•	aqua3 OS Explorer 180 Oxford, Witney & Woodstock
•START / FINISH•	Grid reference: SP 653141
•DOG FRIENDLINESS•	On lead across farmland where there might be cattle
•PARKING•	Room to park by windmill
•PUBLIC TOILETS•	None on route

BACKGROUND TO THE WALK

After successfully holding up the night mail train from Glasgow to London in the early hours of Thursday 8 August 1963 (▶ Walk 7), the Great Train Robbers journeyed 27 or so miles (43.4km) west, across country to a farm near the village of Brill. This was to be their hideout, where they could lay low for a day or two after the robbery.

Remote Hideaway

Leatherslade Farm was just what they wanted – remotely situated on high ground and well away from the road. The men chose the site in the same way that the Romans and the people of the Iron Age chose their hilltop settlements – so they could spot any sign of an approaching enemy. Initially they considered using a fleet of high-powered 3.8 litre engined Jaguars as getaway cars. That way they could be back in London in an hour. But driving at high speed through Buckinghamshire's country lanes in the middle of the night was perhaps not the wisest option.

After careful consideration, they hit upon the idea of looking for a suitable hideout within half an hour's drive of the bridge. In June the men spotted a farm advertised in the local press and after viewing it, made an offer of £5,550, which was accepted. The owners moved out at the end of July and a week later, on the morning of Tuesday 6 August, members of the gang began to arrive at the farm. By midnight the following evening they were ready for action.

A Clean Sweep

They returned to Leatherslade Farm after the train robbery and began digging a hole in the garden to bury the mailbags. They cleaned the farm from top to bottom, wiping down the surfaces and burning all the shoes and clothes that had been worn during the raid. Using several vans to carry the money, the gang eventually left the farm late on the Friday night – nearly 48 hours after the robbery.

The following Monday, a local farm labourer walked up the track to Leatherslade Farm to look at some of his cows. He noticed that the windows had been blacked out. Climbing through the hedge into the yard, he spotted a five-ton army truck in the shed. Somewhat suspicious, he rang the police who were busy taking up to 400 train robbery-related calls a day. Eventually they arrived at the farm and discovered the lorry, two Land Rovers, a half-dug hole and the remains of a bonfire.

Both inside the farm and out the police found numerous clues indicating that this had been the Great Train Robbers hideout. But they needed proof and the gang had removed any incriminating evidence that could link them to the farm – or so they thought. Ronald Biggs had left his prints on a tomato sauce bottle in the kitchen. It was just what the police had been looking for.

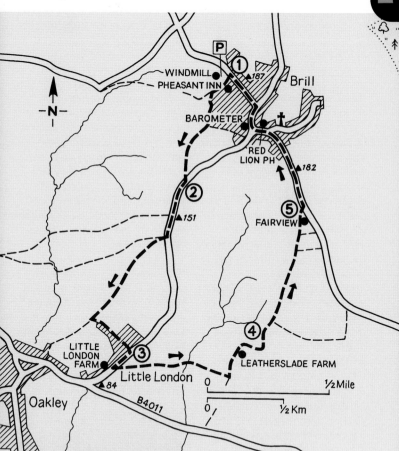

Walk 11 **Directions**

① From the car park go down the lane known as **South Hills**, beside the **Pheasant Inn**, keeping the windmill visible on your right. At a

private lock-up garage and a signpost for **Leyhill**, swing left to join a track. Follow it round to the right to a pair of garages and cross a low stile to the right. A pretty cottage can be seen on the right. Keep to the enclosed footpath and

Walk 11

WHILE YOU'RE THERE

Before starting the walk, take a close look at **Brill Windmill** standing on the edge of the village overlooking the surrounding countryside. The present mill dates from around 1680 and is actually a post mill – a windmill whose whole body revolves around a central post to face the wind. One of the oldest post mills in the country, Brill was last used in 1919 for milling barley. The nearby pits indicate that clay was extracted for use in brick and tile manufacture.

WHAT TO LOOK FOR

Almost at the end of the walk, just beyond the turning to Oakley, is a rarely seen **barometer** in the wall, dating back to 1910. The barometer was erected in memory of Sir Edmund Verney of Claydon House (► Walk 6) in grateful recognition of his devotion to the welfare of the people of Brill and district as county councillor.

a modern house, built to replace the original farmhouse used by the gang during the robbery.

head for two more stiles before crossing rolling grassland. Head towards a large house and a stile to the left of it. Cross over to the road and turn right.

② Pass a public footpath, then look for a bridleway and footpath sign further down on the right and cross into the field at the stile. Head diagonally right down the field to a plank bridge and stile. Aim broadly left down the adjoining field, making for a stile just to the right of the bottom corner. Turn left and follow a footpath through the undergrowth to a cottage. Keep left and bear right after a few paces into **Oakley**. Walk along **Little London Green** to the road and turn right.

③ Take the first path on the left, opposite **Little London Farm**. Head diagonally left in the field, pass under power lines and make for a gateway. Cross the next field to a waymark and galvanised gate and then continue ahead across the next pasture to a stile and track. Bear left and walk up the track towards **Leatherslade Farm**. As you approach the farm gate, take the bridle path to the left of it and skirt the house and outbuildings. This is

④ Once clear of the farmhouse buildings, keep climbing gently, passing a public footpath on the right. Cut between trees and banks of vegetation and make for the next galvanised gate. Continue ahead, with the field boundary on your right. Pass several more footpaths on the right and keep going until you reach a gate in the top boundary. Follow the track ahead to the road by the entrance to a house called **Fairview**.

⑤ Keep left here and walk along the road to **Brill**. Pass the Wesleyan chapel, over to the right across the green is the village church. The **Red Lion** can also be seen at this end of Brill. Pass a turning on the left to Oakley and look for the barometer in the wall. Bear left into **Windmill Street** and return to the car park.

WHERE TO EAT AND DRINK

There are a couple pubs in Brill – the **Red Lion** and the **Pheasant**, which is conveniently situated at the walk's start/finish point. Choose something from the bar menu, perhaps pasta or a burger, or if you need more substantial sustenance the pub offers a range of steak and fish dishes, among other fare.

Hartwell's Green Abode

Combine the pleasure of a walk beside the River Thame with a stroll through the grounds of a hotel with a remarkable history.

•DISTANCE•	5 miles (8km)
•MINIMUM TIME•	2hrs
•ASCENT / GRADIENT•	180ft (55m) ▲ ▲ ▲
•LEVEL OF DIFFICULTY•	👫 👫 👫
•PATHS•	Field and riverside paths, tracks and lanes, 6 stiles
•LANDSCAPE•	Gently rolling farmland and villages south of River Thame
•SUGGESTED MAP•	aqua3 OS Explorer 181 Chiltern Hills North
•START / FINISH•	Grid reference: SP 783123
•DOG FRIENDLINESS•	On lead near Lower Hartwell Farm and alongside Thame
•PARKING•	Space in Eythrope Road, Hartwell
•PUBLIC TOILETS•	None on route

BACKGROUND TO THE WALK

> *'Why wouldst thou leave*
> *calm Hartwell's green abode...*
> *Apician table and Horatian Ode?'*

So wrote Lord Byron on Louis XVIII's departure for France to assume his throne in 1814. Few hotels can boast such a royal connection, but it was in the library of Hartwell House, just outside Aylesbury, that its most famous resident, Louis XVIII, exiled King of France, signed the accession papers to the throne. Louis leased the house for five years, between 1809 and 1814, staying here with his court during the Napoleonic wars. The Queen of France died here during this period and her coffin was taken from Hartwell to Sardinia.

Good Old Boys

One of England's finest stately homes and grandest country hotels, Hartwell House was built for the Hampden and Lee families, ancestors of the American Civil War soldier, General Robert E Lee, during the 17th and 18th centuries. Now a Grade I listed building, the house has many Jacobean and Georgian features, magnificent decorative plasterwork, ceilings and panelling, fine paintings and antique furniture.

The philanthropist Ernest Edward Cook, grandson of tourist pioneer Thomas Cook, who was an important benefactor of the National Trust and National Art Collections Fund, bought Hartwell House and its estate from the Lees in 1938. He was also a founder of the Ernest Cook Trust, which, in the mid-1980s, made Hartwell House and its parkland available to Historic House Hotels for a major restoration and conversion.

Impressive Entrance

The entrance to the house is via a porch flanked by pillars of carved stone, and a carved doorway. Set above all this is a splendid oriel window sitting on intricately embroidered stone corbels. The great hall is an imposing room in English baroque style built by James Gibbs in 1740. The rococo morning room with its decorated ceiling and door cases, the adjoining drawing room and the library, are all Georgian and date from about 1760. The principal dining room is by Eric Throssell and reflects the style of the early 19th-century architect Sir John Soane. Hartwell stands in 90 acres (36ha) of parkland, which was laid out by a pupil of the eminent landscape designer Lancelot 'Capability' Brown. Among the features is a lake spanned by a delightful stone bridge and fed by nearby springs.

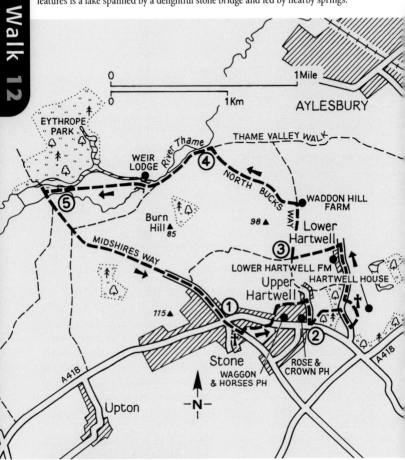

Walk 12 **Directions**

① From the **A418** turn into **Bishopstone Road** and keep to the left of the church. Walk along to the footpath beside **Manor Farm Close** and cross the pasture to a kissing gate leading out to a recreation ground. Pass ornate gate pillars on the left, recalling the men of the village who died in the world wars, and exit to the road by railings.

Cross over to a footpath sign and a gate for **Woodspeen** and follow the drive to a timber garage and shed. Bear right to a gate and follow the path to the road. Turn right, walk up to the **A418** and on the right is the **Rose and Crown**.

② Swing left at the corner and follow the path alongside a stone wall. Head for the road, bear right and walk along to the entrance to **Hartwell House**. Veer left at the

Walk 12

gate pillars and follow the waymarked path through the hotel grounds. Go through a kissing gate, keep the church on your right and the little graveyard on your left. Turn right at the road and pass the Egyptian-style pavilion. Avoid the North Bucks Way running off to the left, pass **Lower Hartwell Farm** and turn left at the footpath. Cross two fields via three stiles and turn right immediately beyond a plank bridge.

③ Skirt the field and make for a stile ahead. Keep the hedge on your left and continue on the **North Bucks Way**, heading towards **Waddon Hill Farm**. Cross a stile, walk ahead alongside timber barns and turn left at the waymark. Follow the track out across the fields to where it eventually it sweeps left. Leave it at this point and go straight on along a path to

a stile. Cross a meadow and head for the **River Thame**. Swing left at the riverbank to a gate and join the **Thame Valley Walk**.

④ After about 60yds (55m) the path reaches a second gate at the point where the river begins a wide loop away to the right. Follow the stream to the next gate and rejoin the riverbank. Follow the **Thame**, avoiding the bridleway branching away from the river, and continue on the waymarked trail. Make for a footbridge and weir, on the opposite bank is an ornate lodge. Join a straight concrete track and follow it towards trees.

⑤ Once in the trees, the Thame can be seen immediately on the left. To the right is the parkland of **Eythrope**. Bear right at the next junction to glimpse the park. To continue the walk, keep left and follow the tarmac drive. Begin a moderate lengthy ascent before reaching the houses of **Stone**.

WHAT TO LOOK FOR
The **Hartwell Estate** boasts many treasures. The bridge over the lake, erected at the end of the 19th century, is the central span of old Kew Bridge built in the 18th century by James Paine, but dismantled in 1898. Outside the main door of the house stands an equestrian statue of Frederick, Prince of Wales and in nearby Weir Lane is an Egyptian-style pavilion over a spring, dating back to 1851. **Eythrope Park**, on the north bank of the Thame, and once the country seat of the Dormer and Stanhope families, has an interesting history. The river was used to create a lake and Sir William Stanhope, who died in 1772, enlarged the house and decorated the garden. The Waddesdon Manor Estate later acquired the park and in the 1880s Miss Alice de Rothschild had a pavilion erected by the lake. The house was dismantled in the early 19th century.

Chequers – Country Seat of our Chosen Leaders

Explore the rolling Chilterns and savour glimpses of a famous Elizabethan mansion – rural retreat of the Prime Minister.

•DISTANCE•	5 miles (8km)
•MINIMUM TIME•	2hrs
•ASCENT / GRADIENT•	378ft (115m) ▲▲▲
•LEVEL OF DIFFICULTY•	★★ ★★ ★★
•PATHS•	Field and woodland paths and tracks, stretch of Ridgeway, 9 stiles
•LANDSCAPE•	Chiltern country, a mixture of rolling hills and woodland
•SUGGESTED MAP•	aqua3 OS Explorer 181 Chiltern Hills North
•START / FINISH•	Grid reference: SP 8420696
•DOG FRIENDLINESS•	Under control on Ridgeway and on lead at Butler's Cross, Ellesborough and Great Kimble
•PARKING•	Limited spaces at Butler's Cross
•PUBLIC TOILETS•	None on route

BACKGROUND TO THE WALK

In an age when politicians and world leaders live with the constant threat of terrorist attacks, it is perhaps a little surprising that you can take a country walk through the grounds of Chequers – the Prime Minister's official country seat near Princes Risborough. The Ridgeway cuts across its picturesque parkland, almost like a symbol of our democratic heritage, passing within sight of Chequers and offering superb views of the house and its glorious Chiltern setting.

Weekend Retreat or Veritable Fortress?

But don't be fooled. When the Prime Minister chooses Chequers to host a summit or entertain the Russian President, you can be sure that the security forces will have it sealed like a drum. Surveillance is usually discreet and understated – there might not be armed guards and security barriers as far as the eye can see, but you know you are being watched.

Take a walk in the surrounding countryside and chances are you'll strike up a conversation with people who claim to have seen police combing the woods in search of terrorists or cranks. One couple I met locally told me they had seen two identical convoys of ministerial cars and Special Branch 4x4 vehicles leaving Chequers one winter's day – one presumably carrying the Prime Minister and his staff, the other a possible decoy. Fact or fiction, it all adds to the romance and mystery of Chequers and provides plenty of fodder for writers of political thrillers.

Gifted to the Nation

Built in 1565, the house was given to the nation in 1921 by Viscount Lee of Fareham. He wrote: '...the better the health of our rulers the more sanely they will rule, and the inducement to spend two days a week in the high and pure air of the Chiltern hills and woods will, it is hoped, benefit the nation as well as its chosen leaders'. Lady Mary Grey, sister of the ill-fated Lady Jane, was initially confined here in disgrace by Elizabeth I after marrying Thomas Keys without her consent. Civil War battles were fought in this part of the country and the house contains one of the finest collection of relics from that period, though sadly they are not seen by the public.

Not all Prime Ministers have been impressed by Chequers. Bonar Law disliked the country. Clement Attlee, on the other hand, loved it from the start and even bought a house in the area when he retired. Ramsay McDonald described it as 'this house of comforting and regenerating rest', but it was Churchill, typically, who summed it up best with these words. 'What distinguished guests it has sheltered, what momentous meetings it has witnessed, what fateful decisions have been taken under this roof'.

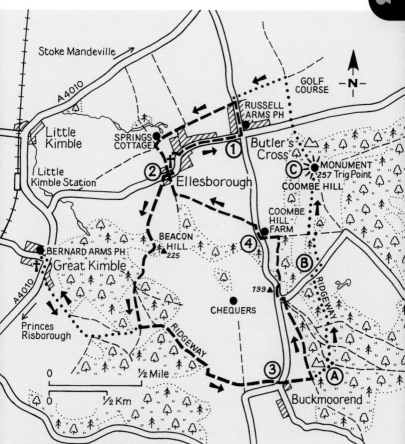

Walk 13 **Directions**

① From **Butler's Cross** follow **Chalkshire Road**, keeping the **Russell Arms** on the right. Walk along to a row of cottages and take the path opposite signposted '**Aylesbury Ring**'. Cross four stiles and pass a path on the right. Continue to a drive on a bend and keep ahead, passing **Springs Cottage**. Ahead of you now are two stiles. Veer left to a further stile, and

WHAT TO LOOK FOR
If you take the spur to Great Kimble for lunch or a relaxing pint, pause to study the superb sign for **St Nicholas Church**, which depicts the patron saint of children. In this church, in 1637, John Hampden announced that he would not pay Ship Money and so took the country a step nearer to the Civil War. The tax had been imposed on ports before the Spanish Armada invasion threat but Charles I's intention to introduce the tax nationally led to an uprising.

Kimble, go through the gate and follow the **Ridgeway** down to the village. To continue the walk, bear left across the field to a kissing gate. Keep woodland on the right and **Chequers** in view across the field. Follow the path to a Ridgeway waymark, cross the field and the drive to the house and continue to a kissing gate.

WHILE YOU'RE THERE
Have a look at **Ellesborough church**. It may be locked but outside, above the porch, are figures indicating it is dedicated to St Peter and St Paul. Look for St Peter's and St Paul's Cottages on the eastern side of the churchyard. There's been a church here for centuries but the present building is Victorian. Past Prime Ministers have worshipped here and even read the lesson.

then swing left and head up the field slope to **Ellesborough church**. Cross a stile into the churchyard and keep to the right of the church. Cross the road to a bus stop and veer right for several paces to a kissing gate.

② Follow the path diagonally up the slope to a stile, sweeping round to the right of **Beacon Hill**. Make for a stile and continue through woodland, up a flight of steps to the edge of the trees. Cross a field at the top, heading for the next wood, and take the track between trees. Cross a track leading to **Chequers**, make for a stile and initially follow the field boundary. After several paces, leave the wood on the left and stride out across the field to a kissing gate. To visit the **Bernard Arms** at Great

WHERE TO EAT AND DRINK
The **Russell Arms** at Butler's Cross is a traditional country inn offering a bar and restaurant. The **Bernard Arms** offers a good quality menu and relaxing surroundings where you can study photographs of several Prime Ministers. John Major and President Yeltsin are pictured with their wives outside the pub in the 1990s. Harold Wilson also called in for a pint on his last Sunday in office in 1976 and was photographed with his wife in the bar.

③ Cross the road and follow the **Ridgeway** through woodland. On reaching a four-way junction, turn left and follow the path along the side of the hill. After ½ mile (800m), a number of paths converge. Turn left at the road, then right where it joins another road. Keep to the right edge and pass a **lodge house**. Follow the path north as the road diverges to the north west. Continue through woodland to a gate. Bear left, leaving the National Trust land by a second gate. Follow the path and drive to the road by **Coombe Hill Farm**.

④ Turn right, cross over to a barrier and join a long path half right up a large field. Bear right at a track, following it to the road opposite **Ellesborough church**. Enter the churchyard, keep to the right of the church and make for an iron gate. Pass some cottages on the left, go downhill to the pavement and return to **Butler's Cross**.

Coombe Hill Viewpoint

Follow woodland paths to a lofty monument for views in all directions.
See map and information panel for Walk 13

•DISTANCE•	6 miles (9.7km)
•MINIMUM TIME•	2hrs 45min
•ASCENT / GRADIENT•	165ft (50m) ▲▲▲
•LEVEL OF DIFFICULTY•	🚶🚶 🚶🚶 🚶

Walk 14 Directions (Walk 13 option)

At the four-way junction where Walk 13 turned left, just after Point ③, go straight ahead. This leads to a slightly longer alternative route back to Butler's Cross. Go straight ahead up the steep slope through the wood. Bear left at the next waymarked **Ridgeway** junction (Point Ⓐ), swinging right after several paces at the next sign. Keep to the left of a disused pit in the woodland and follow the waymarks through the trees. Cross a bridleway and keep right at a Ridgeway and footpath waymark. Continue through the trees and then alongside wooden fencing to a stile. Bear immediately left and make for the next stile and kissing gate, out to the road, Point Ⓑ.

Turn right and walk along to a cottage with white fencing. Bear left and follow the Ridgeway through the trees. Turn left at the next path junction, and then swing right after several paces, avoiding the path running straight ahead, down the hill. Follow the path to the monument on top of **Coombe Hill** (Point Ⓒ), with magnificent views along this stretch over a sizeable

area of Buckinghamshire. **Chequers** and the houses of **Ellesborough** are clearly seen from this breezy viewpoint. Gliders often swoop silently into view in the skies above.

Coombe Hill represents the highest open space in the Chilterns, so it's hardly surprising that this lofty viewpoint, 843ft (257m) above sea level, was chosen to erect a splendid memorial to the men of Buckinghamshire who died during the Boer War (1899–1902). The monument, seen clearly from the grounds of Chequers, was erected by public subscription in 1904, under a resolution proposed by the Lord Lieutenant of the county. The ill-fated memorial was struck by lightning in 1938 and later rebuilt. There was more bad luck in 1972 when the bronze tablet attached to the memorial was stolen. A stone one replaces it.

Keep the monument behind you and descend steeply to the road at the foot of the hill. Cross over and follow the clearly waymarked path across the immaculate fairways of **Ellesborough Golf Club**. Walk ahead to a stile, skirt a field to the next stile on the left and follow the path across the field to the road, crossing two stiles. Turn left and return to the start of the walk.

Walk 15

End of the Line at Chesham

Discover the delights of the little-known Chess Valley before returning to Chesham by tube.

•DISTANCE•	5 miles (8km)
•MINIMUM TIME•	2hrs 15min
•ASCENT / GRADIENT•	165ft (50m) ▲▲▲
•LEVEL OF DIFFICULTY•	🚶🚶 🚶🚶 🚶
•PATHS•	Roads, field and woodland paths and tracks, 8 stiles
•LANDSCAPE•	Unspoiled farmland and woodland scenery of Chess Valley
•SUGGESTED MAP•	aqua3 OS Explorer 181 Chiltern Hills North
•START / FINISH•	Grid reference: SP 960016
•DOG FRIENDLINESS•	On lead in Chesham,Latimer and where there may be livestock, under control elsewhere
•PARKING•	Chesham tube
•PUBLIC TOILETS•	Chesham tube and Chalfont and Latimer tube

Walk 15 Directions

If you're not familiar with the county of Buckinghamshire, it's something of a surprise to arrive at a small country town and find signs for the London Underground – the instantly recognisable circle with a line running through it. At Chesham's charming little station you can board a tube train and travel 25 miles (40.2km) to Aldgate in the City of London via places like Finchley Road, Northwood Hills, Wembley Park and Pinner – the heart of Metroland.

Chesham lies at the end of a branch of the Metropolitan Line, which opened in 1889. Together with nearby Amersham, it's one of London Underground's furthest outposts. Work began on extending what was then known as the St John's Wood Line beyond central London during the latter years of the 19th century. By the mid-1880s the railway had become known as

the Metropolitan, running 17½ miles (28km) from Baker Street. The plan was to continue the line all the way to Aylesbury, but financial problems restricted its extension at that time to Chesham.

> **WHERE TO EAT AND DRINK** ⓘ
>
> There are no pubs on the rural stretches of the walk, but Chesham offers plenty of choice – including the **Last Post** and the **Cock Tavern**, which has a wide-ranging menu, with everything from pizza to jumbo sausage and toasted sandwiches.

Most of the land for the new sections of railway was acquired from the Duke of Bedford and Lord Chesham, but the land for the final half mile (800m) of the Chesham branch was presented to the railway by local residents to enable a station to be built in the centre of the town instead of on the outskirts, as was originally planned. In May 1889 the people of Chesham were invited to inspect the branch and afterwards entertained to a banquet. Seven weeks later, the line from

Rickmansworth to Chesham was opened. For the next three years, until the main line from Chalfont and Latimer Station to Amersham and Aylesbury was opened in 1892, Chesham was the Metropolitan's most northerly terminus.

Turn left out of the station to join the **Chess Valley Walk**. The delightful old signal box can be seen from the path. Bear right at the waymark and walk down to **Trinity Baptist Church**. Cross the main road and follow the way through **Meades Water Gardens** to reach the road by a roundabout. Make for **Moor Road** on the far side and pass beneath the railway. When the road sweeps right, go straight on along a tarmac path. Swing right at the next footbridge and rejoin the road.

Pass a swimming pool and go straight over at the next junction, following the trail between the river and a recreation ground. Join the road by a weir and maintain direction along **Latimer Road**. When it swings right at a bridge, veer off to the left to a stile,

---

signposted 'Blackwell Hall'. Cross four stiles to reach the road. Swing left, passing **Blackwell Farm**, and continue ahead on a track as the lane sweeps left. On reaching farm outbuildings, go straight ahead.

There are two tracks running parallel across the fields. Keep to the left track, go through a gate and continue over farmland, crossing two stiles to reach a gate leading into the wood. Follow the path uphill, ignore a path on the right and make for the woodland edge. Skirt the field, keeping the trees on your right and head for a kissing gate. Walk towards a white gate for several paces, looking for a stile in the left boundary, out to the road.

Turn right, pass the entrance to **Parkfield Latimer** and follow the road down to the **Old Rectory** and the entrance to **Latimer House**, now the offices of Price Waterhouse Coopers. Continue down the road to the next entrance to the house and just beyond it join a tarmac drive running down into the valley. Down by the weir the view to the north is dominated by the façade of Latimer House. When the drive forks, go through the gate ahead and across the pasture to the road.

Cross over to a kissing gate and follow the wide path up the field slope towards woodland. Bear right to pass a stile and about 75yds (69m) beyond it, veer left and climb between the trees. Cross a wide track and head for a house. Keep to the right of it and join a drive leading to a road. Follow **Chenies Avenue**, cross **Elizabeth Avenue** and head down to a junction. Bear left and walk along to the **Chalfont and Latimer Station** to catch the tube back to Chesham.

WHAT TO LOOK FOR ⓘ

Latimer House, once the home of Lord Chesham and now a conference centre, was originally an Elizabethan manor house, but was badly damaged by fire during the 1830s. The house was later restored and during the Second World War it became an interrogation centre. Later, the house was used as the headquarters of the Joint Services Staff College, then the National Defence College. A short distance from Latimer Station lies the entrance to **Beel House**, the former home of the film star Dirk Bogarde (1921–99). It was here that he entertained some of Hollywood's most famous celebrities, including Judy Garland, Ava Gardner, Gregory Peck and Elizabeth Taylor.

Jordans and its Waters of Peace

Visit a Quaker settlement and museum recalling the life of a famous poet.

•DISTANCE•	6¾ miles (10.9km)
•MINIMUM TIME•	2hrs 45min
•ASCENT / GRADIENT•	98ft (30m) ▲▲▲
•LEVEL OF DIFFICULTY•	林 林 林
•PATHS•	Paths across farmland and some road walking, 12 stiles
•LANDSCAPE•	Undulating farmland and woodland on edge of Chilterns
•SUGGESTED MAP•	aqua3 OS Explorer 172 Chiltern Hills East
•START / FINISH•	Grid reference: SU 991937
•DOG FRIENDLINESS•	On lead where signs request it and at Jordans
•PARKING•	Car park off main street, almost opposite church
•PUBLIC TOILETS•	In main street, near Milton's Cottage

BACKGROUND TO THE WALK

A simple stone in a quiet burial ground in the Chilterns marks the grave of outspoken Quaker William Penn (1644–1718). There is nothing here that indicates what this man achieved in his lifetime – the founding of Pennsylvania in 1682.

Penn's Last Resting Place

Penn had a difficult life. Imprisoned on several occasions for speaking out against the religious principles of the day, he always remained loyal to his beliefs. It was Penn who secured the release, in 1686, of almost 2,000 people imprisoned on religious grounds. He and his two wives, Hannah and Gulielma, together with ten of their 16 children, are interred in the burial ground beside the historic Meeting House. The house was built by Quakers in 1688 as soon as the Declaration of Indulgence, issued by James II, ended the persecution of non-conformists. Step inside and, looking at the plain wooden benches and the walls decorated with portraits, it is as if time has stood still.

Jordans Farm

During the 17th century Old Jordans Farm, next door to the Meeting House, was a meeting place of the early pioneering Quakers, as well as the scene of religious persecution. The farm, whose history can be traced back to 1618, was inherited by William Russell, son of Thomas Russell, the sitting tenant. He eventually bought the freehold – the deed, complete with the thumb-prints of the principals and witnesses, now hangs at Old Jordans. Over 300 years ago William Penn worshipped here with fellow Quakers, but meetings were frequently broken up by order of the local court. Undeterred, these people continued to spread their message, often travelling to the far-flung corners of the country.

Old Jordans remained in Quaker hands until the early years of the 18th century. By 1910 the Society of Friends discovered that the farm, now virtually derelict, was up for sale. They acquired it the following year, members carrying out extensive improvements and adding a wing in 1920. In recent years a new building has replaced the old refectory.

Mayflower Timbers

On the south side of the garden lies the Mayflower Barn, originally the main barn of Old Jordans farm and, like many Buckinghamshire barns, built of old ships' timbers. The barn, built the same year the *Mayflower* was broken up, is said to contain timber from the ship. The dining room door at Old Jordans is also believed to come from the vessel which carried the Pilgrim Fathers to America.

Today, Old Jordans is a Quaker guest house and conference centre. It attracts visitors from all over the world and has been called a 'well where men come to draw waters of peace'.

Walk 16 Directions

① From the car park turn right and walk through the village. After ¾ mile (1.2km), bear right into **Back Lane**, swinging left after a few paces. Keep left at the fork, avoid a stile in the boundary and continue to a wide gap in the hedge, just before the field corner. Cross into the adjoining field and continue to maintain the same direction, following the path for about 60yds (55m) to a stile. Keep ahead in the next field, with the hedge on your left, and make for the next stile. Follow the clear path across fields and between trees until you reach a stile and waymark.

② Turn left and skirt the field to a gate and stile. At this point the path runs through trees to the next stile beyond which is a drive. Follow it alongside **New Barn Farm** to the road. Turn left and left again at the junction. Bear right just beyond a left bend and follow the waymarked track to **Willow Court Stables**. Go through a kissing gate and follow the fenced path alongside paddocks.

WHAT TO LOOK FOR ⓘ

The little estate office at **Jordans** recalls the life and work of Fred Hancock, secretary of the village for 25 years. A plaque on the wall draws your attention to his achievements, pointing out that he worked tirelessly to realise the ideals of the founders, devoting himself wholeheartedly to the maintenance and welfare of the village.

---

③ On reaching a path crossroads, turn right and pass through a kissing gate, under power cables. Make for a stile and gate and cross the recreation ground. Continue ahead, cross the drive to **Manor Farm** and follow the wide tree-lined path. Head for a path junction and go straight ahead between houses. Cross **Copse Lane** and follow **Seer Green Lane** into the village. Keep ahead to the junction and turn right towards **Seer Green**. Pass **Old Jordans Quaker Guest House** and follow the road down to the **Meeting House**.

④ Turn left into **Welders Lane** and pass the entrance to a youth hostel. Continue along the lane to a track on the left, signposted 'Grove Farm'. Walk along to a stile on the left, just before a private property sign, and head diagonally across a paddock, passing beneath power cables. Cross four stiles, then turn right and follow the fenced path to a

---

WHERE TO EAT AND DRINK ⓘ

The **Merlin's Cave** pub in Chalfont St Giles offers the likes of liver and bacon, chilli con carne, bangers and mash, sandwich platters, toasted sandwiches and oven-baked jacket potatoes. Morning coffee, afternoon tea and dinner are available at **Old Jordans**.

---

galvanised gate. Keep along the woodland edge, pass a path on the right and continue to a junction by the corner of a wire fence.

⑤ Swing right and pass through the trees to a stile by the road. Cross over and follow an enclosed path. Eventually you'll come down to a track by a bungalow called **Brymavic**. Cross over and continue on the path as it skirts a bowling green, playing fields and a recreation ground. Look for a path in the corner and keep to the right of a school. Go down to the road, turn right and return to the car park in **Chalfont St Giles**.

WHILE YOU'RE THERE ⓘ

John Milton (1608–74), one of England's greatest poets, settled in **Chalfont St Giles** in 1665, fleeing the plague in London to finish *Paradise Lost* (1665). He chose a cottage in the main street, and today his home and garden are open to the public. Have a look around the village and you may well recognise it as Walmington-on-Sea in the film version of *Dad's Army* (1971).

Disraeli's Des Res at Hughenden Manor

Visit the home of a famous British statesman on this scenic Chiltern walk.

•DISTANCE•	7 miles (11.3km)
•MINIMUM TIME•	2hrs 45min
•ASCENT / GRADIENT•	280ft (85m) ▲▲▲
•LEVEL OF DIFFICULTY•	👫 👫 👫
•PATHS•	Field, woodland and parkland paths, some roads, 5 stiles
•LANDSCAPE•	Heart of Chilterns, north of High Wycombe
•SUGGESTED MAP•	aqua3 OS Explorer 172 Chiltern Hills East
•START / FINISH•	Grid reference: SU 826952
•DOG FRIENDLINESS•	On lead around West Wycombe and Downley, signs at various points request dogs be on lead or under control
•PARKING•	Car park by church and mausoleum at West Wycombe
•PUBLIC TOILETS•	Hughenden Manor, West Wycombe House

BACKGROUND TO THE WALK

Looking at Hughenden Manor's delightful setting on the slope of a hill and surrounded by woods and unspoiled parkland, it's not difficult to see why Benjamin Disraeli, Queen Victoria's favourite Prime Minister, chose it as his country home in 1848.

Born in 1804, the baptised son of a Spanish Jew, Disraeli was clever and ambitious. Fiercely political, his main objectives in life were to further the cause of the workers, popularise the monarchy and foster the might, unity and glory of the British Empire. His greatest political rival was the Liberal leader William Gladstone who disliked Disraeli's imperialism and his grand notions of empire.

Queen's Favourite

It was Disraeli who turned Queen Victoria against Gladstone, forging a close association with the Monarch at a time when she most needed the trust and support of others. After her beloved Albert died in 1861, Victoria withdrew from public life to mourn his loss. As the years passed, she became an increasingly distant and reclusive figure – isolated from her family and her subjects. Benjamin Disraeli coaxed her back, winning her trust and giving her the confidence she needed to continue as Queen. Towards the end of his life, he had become one of her closest confidants.

By the time he and his wife, Mary Anne, moved to Hughenden, Disraeli was already an established novelist as well as a significant figure in British politics. Having been elected leader of the Conservative Party in the House of Commons, it was clear he was destined for higher office. Disraeli became Chancellor of the Exchequer in Lord Derby's three successive ministries and Prime Minister in the 1860s and 70s. Widowed in 1872, he was created Earl of Beaconsfield four years later, remaining at Hughenden until his death in 1881.

When Disraeli purchased Hughenden Manor, it was a white-painted, three-storeyed Georgian building of simple, unfussy design. The house was given a Gothic flavour by the architect E B Lamb in 1862, and the west wing was added by Disraeli's nephew, Coningsby.

Now in the care of the National Trust, Hughenden contains most of Disraeli's books, pictures and furniture. There are even manuscripts and various letters from Queen Victoria who spent some time in Disraeli's study after his funeral. The display case in the Disraeli Room has a copy of Prince Albert's printed speeches and addresses, given to Disraeli by Queen Victoria in gratitude for his moving speech in the House of Commons following the Prince Consort's death.

Walk 17 Directions

① From the car park pass to the immediate right of the **church**. Continue to the **mausoleum** and

line up with the **A40** down below. Take the grassy path down the hillside, avoid the path on the right, make your way down to a fork, keep right to a flight of steps and descend to the road. Bear left and

Walk 17

pass **Church Lane** on the right. Take the next path on the right and keep to the right-hand boundary of the field. Look for a stile and maintain the same direction down to a stile by the road.

② Cross over, make for a gate, pass under the railway and, at the field, go straight ahead keeping to the right of the fence. Follow the path to a stile, cross a track and continue up the slope. Make for two stiles by a gate and some barns. Join a lane, swing right at the waymark and follow the ride through woodland. Eventually you reach a stile beyond which the path crosses a field.

③ On reaching a track, turn right and cut through the wood. Veer left at the fork and head for the road. Bear left into **Downley**. Turn left for the pub or right to continue the walk. Pass some houses and when the track bends left, go straight on for a few paces, veering left at the waymark. Cross the common,

following the path through clearings and into trees. On reaching a National Trust sign, turn sharp left and follow the path through the woods. Avoid the path on the left and follow the white arrows. Pass a gate and continue ahead, up the moderately steep slope to a junction.

④ Keep right and follow the path to a track. Swing left to visit **Hughenden Manor** or right to continue the walk. Follow the path through parkland and make for tree cover. Bear immediately left, up the slope through the trees. Look for a house and turn right at the road. Pass the **Bricklayers Arms** and go straight over at the junction.

⑤ Keep ahead through the trees to a housing estate. Go forward for several paces at the road, bearing right at the first footpath sign. Follow the path as it bends left and runs down to a junction. Swing left for several steps, then veer right by some houses, heading down through trees to a galvanised gate. Take the sunken path to the right of it, follow it down to a fork and continue ahead. Head for a lane and follow it towards **West Wycombe**. Cross **Bradenham Road** and walk ahead into the village. Turn right into **West Wycombe Hill Road** and head uphill to the car park.

Walk 18

Turville on TV

Climb into glorious woods and enjoy views you may find familiar.

•DISTANCE•	3 miles (4.8km)
•MINIMUM TIME•	1hr 30min
•ASCENT / GRADIENT•	150ft (45m) ▲▲▲
•LEVEL OF DIFFICULTY•	🚶 🚶🚶 🚶🚶
•PATHS•	Field and woodland paths, some road walking, 9 stiles
•LANDSCAPE•	Rolling Chiltern countryside, farmland and woodland
•SUGGESTED MAP•	aqua3 OS Explorer 171 Chiltern Hills West
•START / FINISH•	Grid reference: SU 767911
•DOG FRIENDLINESS•	On lead around Turville and Skirmett and across farmland
•PARKING•	Small parking area in centre of Turville
•PUBLIC TOILETS•	None on route

BACKGROUND TO THE WALK

A visit to the delightful Chiltern village of Turville leaves you with the impression that you may have been here before – not in reality perhaps, but in the private world of fantasy and imagination. It's more than likely you have been to Turville without ever leaving the comfort of your armchair. Puzzled? Then look a little closer as you begin this walk and you'll find the answer is quite simple.

Turville is one of Britain's most frequently used film and television locations. Its picturesque cottages and secluded setting at the bottom of a remote valley make it an obvious choice for movie makers and production companies. Over the years the village has featured regularly both on the large and small screen. Two notable productions in recent years have brought Turville to the attention of a new generation of television audiences. The BBC comedy *The Vicar of Dibley*, starring Dawn French in the title role, is filmed in the village and the tiny cottage by the entrance to the church doubles as the vicar's home.

Back in 1998, the village was extensively used in the award-winning ITV drama *Goodnight Mister Tom* with the late John Thaw. This delightful wartime story was an immediate hit and Turville's classic village 'Englishness' was the programme's cornerstone.

Goodnight Mister Tom may have been set during the Second World War, but one of Britain's most famous propaganda movies, filmed at Turville, was actually shot during it. *Went the Day Well*, based on a short story by Grahame Greene, dates back to 1942 and illustrates how a small English village is captured by German fifth columnists. Several locals and ex-residents of Turville recall how they moved props on a handcart and pushed rolls of barbed wire on cartwheels, which were used in the film as blockades. The Old School House, by the green, was the local police station in the story.

Overlooking the village is Cobstone Mill, an 18th-century smock mill, which has also played a key part in various productions. The windmill was used in a 1976 episode of *The New Avengers* television series in which Purdey and Gambit, played by Joanna Lumley and Gareth Hunt, drive through the village in a yellow MGB, chasing a helicopter that lands by the windmill. Cobstone Mill was also used in the delightful children's film classic *Chitty Chitty Bang Bang* (1968), starring Dick Van Dyke as eccentric Caractacus Potts, who transforms an old racing car into a wondrous flying toy. The family lived in the windmill.

COBSTONE MILL

Turville

①

BULL & BUTCHER PH

⑤

Fingest

High Wycombe

Mousells Wood

Little Frieth

Frieth

②

POYNATTS FARM

③

Skirmett

COBS COTTAGE

④

FROG INN

Great Wood

▲175

CHILTERN WAY

165▲

▲170

ST KATHERINE'S

Ⓐ

▲60

COLSTROPE FARM

Ⓒ

Rockwell End

Hamble Brook

Great Wood

Pheasant's Hill

HUTTON'S FARM

Ⓑ

MANOR HOUSE

120▲

↑N

Hambleden

STAG & HUNTSMAN INN

1 Mile

1 Km

Walk 18

Walk 18 Directions

① Take the lane just to the left of the church entrance, with **Sleepy Cottage** on the corner. Pass **Square Close Cottages** and the village school before continuing on the **Chiltern Way** through a tunnel of trees. Climb gently to a gate and keep ahead along the field edge to a waymark in the boundary. Branch half left at this point, heading diagonally down the field to a stile.

② Cross the road to a further stile and follow the track through the trees, passing a gas installation on the right. Pass a bench on the left before breaking cover from the trees. Avoid a path branching off to the right and continue up the field slope to the next belt of trees. **Turville** and its windmill are clearly seen over to the left. Enter the woodland and keep left at the junction. Follow the clear wide path as it contours round the slopes, with the ground, dotted with beech trees, rippling away to the left. Descend the hillside, keeping to the woodland edge. Follow the fence and bear left at the next corner, heading to a stile by **Poynatts Farm**.

③ Walk along the drive to the road, bear right and enter **Skirmett**. On the right is **Cobs Cottage** and next door to it is the aptly-named **Ramblers**. Pass the **Frog Inn** and

follow the road south to the next junction. An assortment of houses, a telephone box and a post box line the route. Turn left, pass a stile on the right and walk along to the next left footpath. Follow the field edge to a bungalow and stile, cross over to a drive and make for the road.

> **WHERE TO EAT AND DRINK**
> Though quite expensive, the **Bull and Butcher** at Turville at the start/finish of the walk is an ideal place for refreshment. The **Frog Inn** at Skirmett provides a good selection of home-cooked dishes and bar meals. There's a real fire, family room and garden.

④ Bear right, heading out of the village to the junction with **Watery Lane**. 'Except for access' signs can be seen here now. Look for the stile and footpath immediately to the right of it. Cross the field to a stile in the corner and make for the boundary hedge ahead in the next field. Cross the stile and head diagonally right to a hedge by some houses. Once over the stile, take the road opposite, signposted 'Ibstone and Stokenchurch'.

> **WHAT TO LOOK FOR**
> Some of the best **views of the Chilterns** can be enjoyed on this scenic walk. The chalk hills are thick with beech woods, which makes walking here a joy at any time of the year, and wherever you look there are dry valleys, hidden combes and dramatic escarpments.

> **WHILE YOU'RE THERE**
> Visit Turville's **Church of St Mary the Virgin**. There was a church here in the 12th century, but it is not clear if there was one on this site before that. The first vicar of Turville recorded on the roll in the porch was a Benedictine monk who came here from St Albans in 1228. The squat tower dates from about 1340.

⑤ Walk up the road for about 120yds (110m) and swing left at the first waymarked junction. Follow the **Chiltern Way** between trees, offering teasing glimpses of the Chilterns themselves. Cross a stile and head diagonally down the field towards **Turville**. Make for a track and follow it to the **village green**.

On Location in Hambleden

Opt for a long loop and head for another movie village.
See map and information panel for Walk 18

•DISTANCE•	8¾ miles (14.1km)
•MINIMUM TIME•	3hrs 30min
•ASCENT / GRADIENT•	215ft (95m) ▲▲▲
•LEVEL OF DIFFICULTY•	杰杰 杰杰 杰杰

Walk 19 Directions
(Walk 18 option)

Near the road junction at the southern end of Skirmett, close to **Stud Farm** and between Points ③ and ④, look for a stile and follow the **Chiltern Way**, crossing six stiles to reach a house, Point Ⓐ.

Keep to the left of the house and follow the path through the trees. Keep alongside a hedge, heading towards houses. Cross the field and continue on a track. Go straight on at the road, passing **Colstrope Farm** on the left. Look for a gate on the right bend. Continue ahead to a gate and keep the field edge on your right. Head for a gate and continue, with the field edge now on your left. Make for **Pheasant's Hill** through several gates. Cross a drive to a gate and continue beside a paddock. Ahead lies a stile and gate. Cross the next field, go through a gate and veer left to another. Swing right on the road into **Hambleden**.

Like nearby Turville, this has become a favourite with film makers and television producers. The Walt Disney movie *101 Dalmatians* (1996) was filmed here, as were *Sleepy Hollow* (1999) and *The Avengers* (1998). Hambleden was also used in the television adaptation of Joanna Trollope's novel *A Village Affair* (1989).

Stop off at the **Stag and Huntsman** pub, and then retrace your steps, keeping the church on the left and the manor on the right. At Point Ⓑ pass pairs of cottages and bear right where there is a footpath sign on the left. Follow the track up the hill through the trees, and keep ahead between fields. Pass a stile on the left and continue towards outbuildings at **Hutton's Farm**. Bear sharp left just before them and cross a stile. Follow the track into woodland. Keep left at the fork, cross a track and continue ahead on a grassy path. Cross a stile and keep right at the road.

At Point Ⓒ walk along to **Rockwell End**, swing left here and eventually pass a turning on the right for **Marlow**. Bear left just beyond **St Katherine's**, a retreat, following the tarmac lane to a house with a balcony. The lane dwindles to a path here and descends gradually between trees and bushes. Pass a path running off sharp right and on reaching the road, keep left. Walk down to the path on the right, skirt the field and rejoin Walk 18 at Point ④.

Walk 20

The Meandering Thames at Marlow

Enjoy a pleasant mix of town and country on this attractive riverside walk.

•DISTANCE•	4 miles (6.4km)
•MINIMUM TIME•	1hr 30min
•ASCENT / GRADIENT•	Negligible
•LEVEL OF DIFFICULTY•	
•PATHS•	Pavements, paved paths, lane, byway, field and meadow path, tow path, 1 stile
•LANDSCAPE•	Thames Valley townscape and meadows
•SUGGESTED MAP•	aqua3 OS Explorer 172 Chiltern Hills East
•START / FINISH•	Grid reference: SU 849865
•DOG FRIENDLINESS•	On lead in Marlow and under control on Thames Path
•PARKING•	Car parks in Pound Lane and Oxford Road, off West Street
•PUBLIC TOILETS•	Behind Waitrose at river end of High Street

Walk 20 Directions

A stroll through the streets of Marlow reveals many buildings of architectural and historic interest. From the **tourist information centre** turn right and make for the junction at the top of the **High Street**. Bear left into **West Street**, by the **Crown**.

This popular hostelry dates back to 1807 and was originally built as the town's Market House, replacing a previous wooden building. Up on the first floor is an impressive Assembly Room. The original hotel, a renowned coaching inn, stood immediately to the right of the present building and is now shops and offices. The obelisk outside commemorates the Hatfield to Bath turnpike road.

Continue along **West Street** and pass the **Premier Indian Restaurant** (No 31) on the left, the home of

T S Eliot between 1917 and 1920. Further on is **Ye Olde Tuck Shoppe** on the right and just beyond it are **Shelley House** and **Shelley Lodge**.

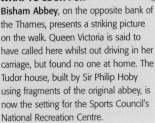

> **WHAT TO LOOK FOR**   ⓘ
>
> **Bisham Abbey**, on the opposite bank of the Thames, presents a striking picture on the walk. Queen Victoria is said to have called here whilst out driving in her carriage, but found no one at home. The Tudor house, built by Sir Philip Hoby using fragments of the original abbey, is now the setting for the Sports Council's National Recreation Centre.

West Street was once the home of the poet Percy Bysshe Shelley, who lived here in 1817, five years before he died. He wrote much of *The Revolt of Islam* (1818) while out boating on the river. At this time his wife Mary, who had married Shelley when she was still a teenager, would be at home working on her classic story *Frankenstein* (first published in 1818). From here the couple moved to Italy.

Walk back along the road, almost to the **Red Lion**, and branch right at the sign for the Town Council Offices and the Thames. Follow the tarmac path and turn right at the next road junction. Head for **Lower Pound Lane** and a byway sign and pass hard tennis courts on the right and a cricket club on the left. Pick your way through the trees, cross a bridge and follow the track as it dwindles to a path.

> ### WHERE TO EAT AND DRINK
> The **Two Brewers** pub, which was a popular haunt of Jerome K Jerome, who supposedly wrote part of *Three Men in a Boat* (1889) here, is a fine watering hole at the end of the walk. The emphasis is on modern European cuisine, and there is a choice of real ales. Relax in the bar or the private dining areas.

Cross a stile, pass a sign for **Quarry Farms** and continue between fields and meadows. Make for **Low Grounds Farm** and keep left at the lane. Head for the Thames, with **Quarry Hill** and **Winter Hill** rising to meet the distant skyline. The buildings of **Temple** can also be seen ahead as you follow the lane towards the tow path. On reaching the river, pause for a good view of **Temple Lock** and the weir. Swing left and follow the **Thames Path** towards **Marlow**.

Further downstream the buildings of **Bisham Abbey** edge into view on the opposite bank. Pass a welcome riverside seat and up ahead you will see Marlow's striking parish church. Pass the council offices and head towards **All Saints** and the town's famous suspension bridge which spans the River Thames, here forming the county boundary between Buckinghamshire and Berkshire.

The bridge, which was completed in 1832, was designed by William Tierney Clark who was inspired by similar bridges he had seen at Hammersmith, in London, and at Budapest. The Marlow suspension bridge is now the only surviving example of his work.

Back in 1965, long before most of today's television soaps were even thought of, the BBC broadcast a drama about daily life in a riverside hotel. The opening shots of *The Flying Swan*, which starred British film actress Margaret Lockwood and her daughter Julia, were filmed across the suspension bridge at the Compleat Angler, one of the south's most famous and exclusive hotels. Omar Sharif, Clint Eastwood and Naomi Campbell are among many celebrities that have stayed at the hotel over the years.

Rebuilt in 1835, All Saints Church occupies a delightful riverside setting at the bottom end of the High Street. There has been a church on this site since Saxon times and inside are many fascinating monuments, including one to Sir Miles Hobart, a parliamentary maverick who, in 1628, locked the door of the House of Commons until various taxation resolutions were passed.

Follow the **High Street**, with Marlow's war memorial and the **George and Dragon** seen over on the right. To visit the Two Brewers pub, take the alleyway on the right, just beyond the church. Head along the **High Street**, cross **Station Road** and look for **Cromwell House** on the right, once the home of Edwin Clark, a noted Victorian engineer. Continue along the street, back to the tourist information centre.

SWC 5/11/09

With P+A.
15/09/11

Burnham's Beautiful Beeches

Enjoy the spacious clearings and sunny glades of a National Nature Reserve,
a welcome green lung in a bustling world.

Walk 21

•**DISTANCE**•	4½ miles (7.2km)
•**MINIMUM TIME**•	1hr 45min
•**ASCENT / GRADIENT**•	150ft (46m) ▲▲ ▲▲
•**LEVEL OF DIFFICULTY**•	👥 👥 👥
•**PATHS**•	Woodland paths and drives, field paths, tracks and stretches of road, 9 stiles
•**LANDSCAPE**•	Dense woodland and some open farmland between Slough and Beaconsfield
•**SUGGESTED MAP**•	aqua3 OS Explorer 172 Chiltern Hills East
•**START / FINISH**•	Grid reference: SU 957850
•**DOG FRIENDLINESS**•	Under effective control within Burnham Beeches and across farmland where there may be livestock
•**PARKING**•	Car park at Burnham Beeches
•**PUBLIC TOILETS**•	Burnham Beeches

BACKGROUND TO THE WALK

Before the Corporation of the City of London bought Burnham Beeches in 1880 for public use and enjoyment, it was described as an area of 'woodland and waste'. Up until that time it had been owned by the Grenville family of Dropmore and on the estate is East Burnham Cottage, where the dramatist Richard Sheridan (1751–1816) and his bride spent their honeymoon after they eloped in 1773. Here, he wrote to a friend: '...were I in a descriptive vein, I would draw you some of the prettiest scenes imaginable'.

Later, in the 19th century, historian George Grote lived here, entertaining such luminaries as Chopin, Mendelssohn, John Stuart Mill and the singer Jenny Lind. It is fascinating to picture these characters strolling among the beeches, admiring their beauty and seeking refuge from the sun.

Nature Reserve
Extending to 600 acres (243ha) and now a National Nature Reserve, Burnham Beeches contains the world's largest collection of ancient beech, with an average age of more than 300 years. The steward of the Hundred of Burnham, one of the original Chiltern Hundreds (Saxon administrative divisions), had an almost impossible job on his hands preventing highway robbery in and around these thick woodlands. The locals were very protective towards the beeches, treating them almost as if they were their own. When the corporation acquired Burnham Beeches, some people protested against the new bylaws in the strongest terms, attacking the keeper and throwing him into a pond.

Burnham Beeches was part of a huge forest that once stretched across the Chilterns in prehistoric times. Much of that woodland has disappeared over the years but the beeches at Burnham continue to remind us of that once thickly-wooded landscape. The beech is one of Britain's most prolific trees and the county of Buckinghamshire is closely associated with what was once nicknamed 'the Chiltern weed'. Native to southern England, the beech has shallow, expanding roots allowing it to thrive on thin soil where many other trees will not grow. Its thick foliage permits only a hint of sunlight to reach the ground beneath it, discouraging the growth of other plants. As a result, a classic beech wood has a floor thickly strewn with its own deep brown, perfectly sculpted leaves. Few of us, when out walking, can resist the temptation to kick our way through them on a glorious autumn day.

Burnham Beeches is perfect for walking. Whilst many people stray little further than the end of the car park, it's very rewarding to plunge deep into the woodland, pausing to admire the wildlife and learn about the process of pollarding along the way. If time allows, you, too, may like to explore the area in greater depth.

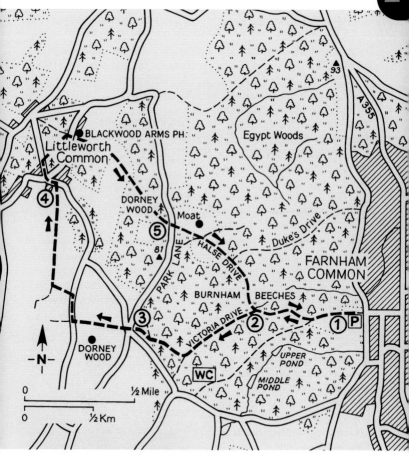

Walk 21 Directions

① Follow the drive away from **Farnham Common**, keeping the car parking area on the left. Pass a refreshment kiosk and veer right at the fork just beyond it. Soon reach a gate where you enter the National Nature Reserve's car-free zone. Follow **Halse Drive** as it curves left and down between trees. At the bottom of the hill swing left into **Victoria Drive**.

Walk 21

WHERE TO EAT AND DRINK ⓘ
There is a **café** at the car park where the walk starts and finishes, open summer and winter weekends. The **Blackwood Arms** at Littleworth Common serves a good range of bar food, including snacks, filled baguettes, scampi, steak and ale pie, double egg, ham and chips and a traditional Sunday roast.

② Follow the broad stony drive between the beeches, avoiding turnings either side of the route, and eventually reach a major junction with a wide path on the left and right. On the right is a large beech tree with 'Andy 6.9.97' carved on the trunk. If you manage to miss the path, you will soon reach the road. Bear right and go up the slope, keep left at the fork and cross several clearings to reach the road at the junction with **Green Lane** and **Park Lane**.

WHILE YOU'RE THERE ⓘ
Learn about the method of **pollarding** trees as you walk through Burnham Beeches. The oldest trees in the area have been pollarded – the branches have been cut at about 8ft (2.5m) from the ground. These branches are often used for firewood and the tree cut again 10–20 years later.

③ Cross the road to a stile and waymark and go straight ahead, keeping the boundary on your left. Make for a stile and descend into the field dip, quickly climbing again to pass alongside the grounds of **Dorney Wood**. Walk ahead to the field corner, cross a stile and turn right at the road. Head for a waymarked footpath on the left and cross the field to a gap in the trees and hedgerow. Turn right and skirt the fields, making for a belt of trees and banks of undergrowth. The

path cuts between two oak trees in the next field before reaching a gap in the hedgerow.

④ Cross a stile out to the road and turn left. Pass **Common Lane** and **Horseshoe Hill** and turn right at the next bridleway. Follow the track through the wood to the next road at **Littleworth Common**. Cross the stile to the right of the **Blackwood Arms** and follow the **Beeches Way**. Beyond the next stile continue ahead alongside the wood, crossing two stiles before following a fenced path. Go through a gate and take the path between the trees of **Dorney Wood**.

WHAT TO LOOK FOR ⓘ
Dorney Wood can be glimpsed from the path. This is the Chancellor of the Exchequer's official country residence, where pre-Budget meetings are held from time to time. The house was built in the 1920s.

⑤ On reaching a stile, cross over to the road and continue on the **Beeches Way**. Make for the next major intersection and keep right along **Halse Drive**. Pass **Victoria Drive** and retrace your steps back to the car park.

Stoke Poges and a Garden Graveyard

Savour the peace and beauty of a cherished ornamental landscape before crossing Gray's Field to a striking monument.

•DISTANCE•	4 miles (6.4km)
•MINIMUM TIME•	1hr 45min
•ASCENT / GRADIENT•	Negligible
•LEVEL OF DIFFICULTY•	
•PATHS•	Semi-residential paths and drives, field tracks and paths, some road walking and stretches over golf courses, 9 stiles
•LANDSCAPE•	Partly residential, interspersed with golf courses and stretches of open countryside
•SUGGESTED MAP•	aqua3 OS Explorer 172 Chiltern Hills East
•START / FINISH•	Grid reference: SU 977825
•DOG FRIENDLINESS•	On lead on golf courses, in Memorial Gardens and churchyard and in residential areas
•PARKING•	Opposite Memorial Gardens
•PUBLIC TOILETS•	Memorial Gardens, closed evenings and weekends

BACKGROUND TO THE WALK

The dawn of the 21st century promises significant changes at Stoke Poges Memorial Gardens. Following a successful application to the Heritage Lottery Fund, money has been made available to restore the gardens over a two-year period, preserving the rich mosaic of trees and shrubs.

A Peaceful Corner

The gardens were founded by Sir Noel Mobbs in 1930 on land that formed part of Stoke Park. Sir Noel's aim was to provide a corner of peace and beauty in an increasingly hectic world, and by the late 1930s they had been designed, landscaped and completed to everyone's satisfaction. The arrival of the motor car brought noise and pollution to the streets of Stoke Poges, but the gardens escaped the intrusive bustle of the 20th century. Today, more than 60 years after they were first landscaped, they remain a haven of tranquillity in a particularly hectic corner of south east England .

The gardens were designed by Sir Edward White, one of Britain's leading landscape architects, and are considered an important example of his work. Dedicated in 1935 as non-denominational memorial grounds, they were acquired by the local authority in 1971 and are registered as Grade II on the English Heritage Register of Parks and Gardens of special interest in England.

Among Flowers and Trees

The Memorial Gardens are regarded as unique in this country – one of the few surviving gems of the pre-war period that have stood the test of time. Even more heartening is that they are still in use today. Those who have loved the gardens in life often choose them as their final resting place. They buy a plot here so their ashes can be interred in beautiful surroundings, where flowers, trees and shrubs reflect the changing seasons and the constant, uninterrupted cycle of life. In short, this is a garden graveyard.

The grounds cover 20 acres (8ha) with 2,000 private gardens, including rock and water gardens, rose gardens, parterre gardens, heath gardens and individual specimen trees and shrubs. There are also formal gardens enclosed by yew hedges and informal gardens surrounded by glorious flowering shrubs. Running through the Memorial Gardens is the main avenue leading down to the colonnade, characterised by columns, water channels, magnolia trees and multi-coloured flower beds.

With over half a century behind them, the gardens have reached the stage where decay and disease are beginning to take their toll. Refurbishment work will restore the character and beauty of the Memorial Gardens for future generations.

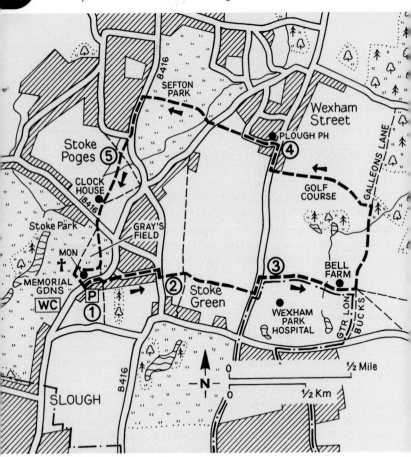

Walk 22 **Directions**

① From the car park, turn right and walk along the road. When the pavement ends, cross over and look

for a waymark and a kissing gate by an oak tree on the right. Go through the gate and follow the path as, initially, it runs parallel with the road. Pass the entrances to various private houses and go

Walk 22

WHILE YOU'RE THERE ⓘ
Take time to look at the **monument to Thomas Gray**, poet and scholar. Gray's *Elegy Written in a Country Churchyard* (1751) has been described as our most famous poem and it was here at Stoke Poges that he composed the final lines. Gray spent much of his time exploring the Buckinghamshire countryside that he dearly loved. The monument was erected in 1799 by John Penn, grandson of William Penn (▶ Walk 16).

through two more gates before the path joins a residential drive – **Duffield Park**. Bear right when you get to the road junction and then take the first footpath on the left, by the sign for Snitterfield House.

② Follow the wide tarmac drive and, avoiding the stile on the left and the turning on the right, continue for several paces to a right-hand stile just before the next sign for the house. Cross the paddock to the stile, make for the boundary, cross a stile and footbridge and then keep along the right edge of the field. Look for a stile by an oak tree in the corner and cross the next field to a hedge gap by the road. Turn left, passing the **hospital** entrance. Just beyond it, on the right, is a private drive sign and an electricity transformer. Bear right here to a stile and gate and follow the track.

③ Cross the next stile after about 50yds (46m) and continue ahead to **Bell Farm**. Pass the outbuildings and keep ahead on a grassy track to a stile and gate. Turn left and follow a bridleway (**Galleons Lane**) to a plank bridge and stile on the left. The walk now crosses a golf course. Cut across the fairways to a wide path and follow it to the club car park. Take the drive, veering right

to a stile by a row of houses and follow the track to the road. Bear right and walk along to the **Plough**.

④ Swing left into **Plough Lane** and when it bends right, go straight on along the public bridleway. Cross the next road to a kissing gate and continue on a waymarked path. Keep ahead, crossing the old driveway to **Sefton Park** and then a golf course before reaching a kissing gate leading out to the road. Turn left and walk along to **Rogers Lane** on the right. Make for the kissing gate on the corner and follow the outline of the path ahead to a second gate.

WHERE TO EAT AND DRINK ⓘ
The **Plough** at Wexham Street is a useful watering hole. Expect traditional home cooking, a Sunday roast and local real ales. There is a beer garden where you may like to relax on a summer's day.

⑤ Branch half right and follow the path towards the **Clock House** and through four more gates before reaching the road. Cross over to a kissing gate and follow the straight path across **Gray's Field**. Keep to the right of the monument and look for the gate leading into the churchyard. Walk through it to the car park.

WHAT TO LOOK FOR ⓘ
Stoke Poges church is usually open and inside you'll find evidence of Saxon, Norman, early Gothic and Tudor influences. At the western end of the church is what is known as the 'Bicycle Window'. The window depicts a figure sitting astride what appears to be some sort of ancient hobby-horse, which he pushes with one foot while playing a trumpet. It looks and sounds comical but, in fact, it was designed as a Second World War memorial.

8/7/04

Walk 23

Dorney Court and England's First Pineapple

Visit one of Buckinghamshire's oldest houses and take a stroll by the Thames.

•DISTANCE•	5 miles (8km)
•MINIMUM TIME•	1hrs 45min
•ASCENT / GRADIENT•	Negligible
•LEVEL OF DIFFICULTY•	
•PATHS•	Roads, firm paths and Thames tow path
•LANDSCAPE•	Lowland Thames valley
•SUGGESTED MAP•	aqua3 OS Explorer 160 Windsor, Weybridge & Bracknell
•START / FINISH•	Grid reference: SU 938776
•DOG FRIENDLINESS•	On lead in Dorney and under control by Thames
•PARKING•	Large car park at Dorney Common
•PUBLIC TOILETS•	None on route

BACKGROUND TO THE WALK

Located in Buckinghamshire's most southerly village, close to the Thames, Dorney Court prides itself on being a genuine medieval village manor house. Motorways and modern housing estates grow ever closer, but the Grade I listed house with its jumble of timber-framed gables has survived intact and unchanged for almost 600 years, looking much the same today as when it was first built.

Fruit and Honey

The village of Dorney stands on a gentle rise in the Thames flood plain and is cut off from the river by spacious meadows where evidence of prehistoric life can be found in the damp peaty soil. The name Dorney means 'island of bumblebees' and the locally produced Dorney Court honey is renowned for its delicate, light flavours.

But it is not just honey for which the house is justly famous. The large carved stone pineapple standing in the corner of the Great Hall commemorates the first pineapple to be grown in England. The story suggests that the top of a pineapple, imported from Barbados, was sliced off at a dinner in the City of London and given to the Earl of Castlemaine's gardener to plant at Dorney Court. The pineapple thrived and was subsequently presented to Charles II in 1661. Nobody can be sure if it really happened but it makes a good story.

Medieval Manor House

Back in the mid-1920s, *Country Life* described Dorney Court as 'one of the finest Tudor manor houses in England'. Few would dispute that label and what endears the house to so many people is its long tradition of continuous family occupation. In fact, Dorney Court has remained in the same family for over 450 years.

The first owner was recorded after the Norman Conquest and after changing hands several times in the 15th century, the house was sold in 1504 for the princely sum of 500 marks. By the middle of the 16th century the manor, together with 600 acres (243ha), was owned by Sir William Garrard, Lord Mayor of London. The Garrards were prosperous grocers, owning land in the Chalfonts area. It is through this family that the town of Gerrards Cross got its name. Sir William Garrard's daughter Martha married Sir James Palmer of Kent and Dorney Court has remained in the Palmer family to this day. One family portraits depicts Jane Palmer, who was born in 1564 and was a forebear of Diana, Princess of Wales. The layout of the house has changed little over the years, though since opening to the public in 1981 work has been undertaken to restore furniture and paintings.

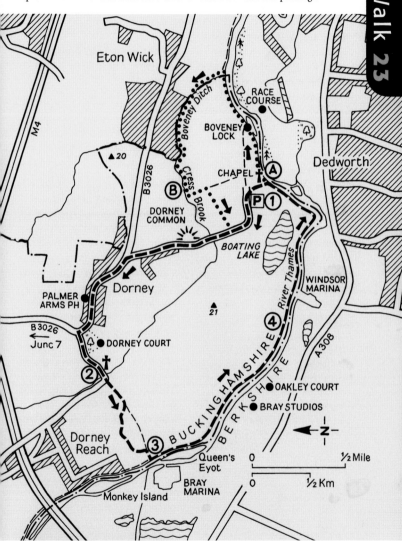

Walk 23 Directions

① From the car park follow the road across **Dorney Common**, towards **Dorney** village. Pass

Wakehams, a timber-framed house with a well situated at the front, and away to the right is a fine view of Windsor Castle and its famous Round Tower. Keep left at the T-junction, cross a cattle grid and join the pavement. Walk through Dorney, keeping the **Palmer Arms** on your right. Bear left into **Court Lane** and pass the entrance to **Dorney Court**. Follow the path parallel to the road and soon reach the **Church of St James the Less**.

② Continue on the path and when the road bends right, go straight ahead at the sign for **Dorney Lake, Park and Nature Reserve**. Keep to the right-hand side of the drive and follow the parallel path as it sweeps away to the right by a plaque and a grove of trees. Further on the path passes over a conveyor belt carrying sand and gravel from the nearby quarry works. Make for some trees and reach the **Thames Path** by a Sustrans waymark.

③ Turn left here and follow the national trail, keeping **Bray Marina** on the opposite bank. Further downstream the imposing cream façade of **Bray film studios** edges into view, its sweeping riverside lawns and weeping willows enhancing the elegant scene. Continue on the leafy **Thames Path** and soon catch sight of **Oakley Court** across the water on the Berkshire bank.

WHERE TO EAT AND DRINK

The **Palmer Arms** at Dorney has been a public house since the 18th century and is said to be haunted by a white lady. The usual snacks and main meals, including jacket potatoes, sandwiches, liver and onions and grilled salmon, are available along with Sunday roast.

④ Beyond the hotel can be seen the cabin cruisers and gin palaces of **Windsor Marina** and next to it lines of caravans and mobile homes overlooking the river. Through the trees on the Buckinghamshire bank is the outline of Eton College's new boathouse and its superb rowing lake. To gain a closer view, briefly follow a path beside the river boathouse and slipway, walk towards the lake and then retrace your steps to the **Thames Path**. On the opposite bank of the river is **Windsor Race Course Yacht Basin** and ahead now is the **Chapel of St Mary Magdalen**. Follow the path alongside the chapel to a kissing gate and about 50yds (46m) beyond it reach a lane. With the **Old Place** opposite and an avenue of chestnut trees on the right, turn left and return to the car park.

WHILE YOU'RE THERE

Dorney Common, still owned by the Lord of the Manor of nearby Dorney Court, has been managed in the same way since medieval times and some local residents are permitted to graze their animals here. After visiting Dorney Court, take time to look at the **Church of St James the Less** at Dorney, which dates from the 13th century. Note the Norman font, the 17th-century gallery, the Garrard tomb and the porch that was built in 1661 to celebrate the birth of Lady Anne Palmer.

WHAT TO LOOK FOR

With its Victorian Gothic façade, **Oakley Court** is an obvious choice for Hammer horror film producers – especially as it lies next door to Bray studios, home of Hammer. The house, now a hotel, has been used in various movie productions, including *The Curse of Frankenstein* (1957) and *The Rocky Horror Picture Show* (1975). The **Chapel of St Mary Magdalen** has been a place of worship since before the Norman Conquest. Parts of it date back to the 12th and 13th centuries and it may well have been used by boatmen when Boveney Lock was a bustling wharf transporting timber from Windsor Forest.

Thames Path to Eton Wick

Follow the river to Boveney Lock within sight of Windsor on this longer loop.
See map and information panel for Walk 23

•DISTANCE•	7 miles (11.3km)
•MINIMUM TIME•	2hrs 45min
•ASCENT / GRADIENT•	Negligible
•LEVEL OF DIFFICULTY•	

Walk 24 Directions (Walk 23 option)

Boveney Lock is said to stand by the site of a former fishery known as Gills Bucks, after the fish traps or bucks owned by Tom Gill. There was a dispute over an unpaid toll here in 1375, thought to be the first reference to a lock on this stretch of the river. There were unsuccessful attempts to create a modern lock here, and it was not until the 1830s that Boveney Lock was opened. The present lock was constructed alongside the earlier one.

At Point Ⓐ keep the **Chapel of St Mary Magdalen** on the left and continue downstream along the **Thames Path**, heading for **Boveney Lock**. **Windsor Racecourse** can be seen over on the Berkshire bank.

The Thames, historically the most important river in Britain, has been used as a highway since early times. A stroll along its banks is surely the best way to appreciate its character, beauty and ever-changing scenery. The Thames Path, officially opened by the Countryside Commission in 1996, is the only long distance national trail in the country to follow a river for its entire length

More than 95 per cent of the trail currently follows the intended route by the Thames, which rises in a Gloucestershire meadow near Cirencester. Despite problems over prohibited access in several places, the Thames Path has come a long way since the 1920s when the concept of providing public access to the countryside led to the eventual designation of the route in 1989.

Continue on the tow path, cross **Boveney Ditch** and bear immediately left at a path junction. The modern Windsor spur road can be seen over on the right, with the magnificent chapel of Eton College rising triumphantly above it. Cross the footbridge by the distinctive Sustrans milepost and veer immediately right. Skirt round the field, keeping the ditch hard by you on the right, and pass a row of houses on the far bank. A waymark edges into view further on as the path follows the **Cress Brook**.

At Point Ⓑ, on reaching the field corner, swing left at the waymark and continue along the perimeter. Look for a path on the right and follow it between fields to a stile. Cross the common to the road and bear left, following it back to the car park at **Dorney Common**.

Walk 25

Royal Windsor

Follow the scenic Thames from Windsor to Datchet and return by train.

•DISTANCE•	2½ miles (4km)
•MINIMUM TIME•	1hr 15min
•ASCENT / GRADIENT•	Negligible ▲▲▲
•LEVEL OF DIFFICULTY•	🚶 🚶 🚶
•PATHS•	Pavements, drive, tow path, path across meadows and playing fields, no stiles
•LANDSCAPE•	Lowland meadows and town outskirts in Thames Valley
•SUGGESTED MAP•	aqua3 OS Explorer 160 Windsor, Weybridge & Bracknell
•START / FINISH•	Grid reference: SU 968772
•DOG FRIENDLINESS•	On lead in Windsor and Datchet, under control elsewhere
•PARKING•	Car park at Riverside Station, Windsor
•PUBLIC TOILETS•	Riverside Station, Windsor

Walk 25 Directions

From Windsor and Eton's **Riverside Station**, turn right to the river bank where you will find the **Donkey House** pub overlooking the Thames. Pass through a set of wrought iron gates and follow **Romney Walk**, restored in 1993 by Windsor Heritage. The land for this footpath was presented by the Southern Railway Company in 1934. To the right are the car park and buildings of Windsor and Eton Riverside Station, where the Royal Waiting Room dates back to 1849. There are good views from here up to Windsor Castle, as well as glimpses of Eton College and its chapel through the trees beyond Romney Island.

> **WHERE TO EAT AND DRINK** ℹ
> Plenty of choice in Windsor, including pubs, restaurants and tea rooms. Try the **Royal Stag** at Datchet. Overlooking the green and once home of Robert Barker, printer to Elizabeth I, the pub offers snacks and more substantial dishes.

Windsor Castle was founded as a fortress by William the Conqueror and has been substantially altered and extended over the centuries. The most recent work undertaken followed the much publicised fire in 1992. During his reign George IV spent nearly £1 million on improving the castle. The dominant feature is its Round Tower, built by Henry II and visible for miles around. Parts of the castle are open to the public, though the state apartments are closed when the Queen is in residence.

With its legendary reputation, Eton College still represents one of this country's great institutes of learning – Gladstone described it as the 'Queen of Public Schools'. On its famous playing fields, according to Wellington, the Battle of Waterloo was won.

In May 1990 the college celebrated a remarkable achievement – its 550th anniversary. It was founded in 1440 by Henry VI who was only 19 at the time – even more remarkable. Eton is modelled on Winchester College, and is the second oldest public school in the country. Originally it accommodated 70 poor scholars who were educated free of charge. The boys of Eton College still wear black tailcoats in mourning for George III, their favourite monarch.

Eton College chapel is similar in many ways to the chapel of Kings College, Cambridge, also founded by Henry VI. It was built between 1449 and 1482 and the chapel you see here today was originally to have been the choir for a much larger, more majestic place of

> ### WHILE YOU'RE THERE ⓘ
> Frogmore House, set in the private Home Park, is renowned for its splendid landscaped garden and 18th-century lake. Queen Victoria wrote of it: 'All is peace and quiet and you only hear the hum of bees, the singing of the birds'. She built a mausoleum for herself and her husband, Prince Albert, in the garden. Frogmore is open to the public on a limited number of days during the year.

worship. The splendid vaulted ceiling and the impressive 15th-century wall paintings are two of the college chapel's most distinguished features. Raised 13ft (4m) above ground, the college chapel is safe from flooding should the Thames burst its banks. Continue ahead on a drive, pass a cottage dated 1898 and a distinctive octagonal building which houses the waterworks for Windsor Castle. On reaching a boatyard, make for the water's edge and walk along the grass tow path beside the river. **Eton College Boathouse** is soon visible on the opposite bank. Pass under the 19th-century **Black Potts railway bridge** and skirt the playing fields on the right. As you

approach the next bridge, veer right to the **Thames Path** sign at the far end of the white railings.

Turn left and follow the pavement over **Victoria Bridge**. Over to the right is the **Home Park**. Bear right on the far side and follow the **Thames Path** through the trees, with delightful views of the Thames and the Home Park beyond. On reaching the road, turn right along the **B470** and then bear left into **Datchet High Street**.

This pleasant riverside village has strong literary associations. The main road to Windsor, at the southern end of the High Street, was the Datchet Lane in William Shakespeare's comedy *The Merry Wives of Windsor* (1602). Falstaff was transported along this road on his way to face the ordeal of a ducking in the Thames. The village is also mentioned in Jerome K Jerome's famous book, *Three Men in a Boat* (1889).

Just before the turn of the century, and again soon after the Second World War, Datchet suffered serious flooding when the swollen Thames caused a pond in the centre of the village to overflow. Several anxious residents were isolated in their homes. Walk along to the green and make your way to the railway station for your return train.

> ### WHAT TO LOOK FOR ⓘ
> Victoria Bridge dates back to the mid-19th century and was partly designed by Prince Albert. Over to the right of it is the Home Park, consisting of 4,000 acres (1,620ha). Closed for security reasons, it was created as a private riverside park for Queen Victoria. The present Queen has come under attack on occasions for not providing public access to the park.

Walk 26

Sunningdale and a Constitutional Crisis

Skirt the grounds of Edward VIII's favourite home on this attractive walk to exclusive Wentworth and Coworth Park.

•DISTANCE•	4 miles (6.4km)
•MINIMUM TIME•	1hrs 45min
•ASCENT / GRADIENT•	Negligible
•LEVEL OF DIFFICULTY•	
•PATHS•	Enclosed woodland paths, estate drive, paths and tracks, path across golf course and polo ground, no stiles
•LANDSCAPE•	Semi-residential area
•SUGGESTED MAP•	aqua3 OS Explorer 160 Windsor, Weybridge & Bracknell
•START / FINISH•	Grid reference: SU 953676
•DOG FRIENDLINESS•	On lead across golf course and polo ground
•PARKING•	On-street parking in Sunningdale village
•PUBLIC TOILETS•	None on route

BACKGROUND TO THE WALK

In the closing weeks of 1936 the newspaper headlines were dominated by one of the saddest and most dramatic chapters in the history of the monarchy – the abdication of Edward VIII, the uncrowned King who chose to give up the throne for the love of a woman, American divorcee Wallis Simpson.

Constitutional Crisis

He knew his decision would provoke the strongest disapproval – that what he wanted to do would be at odds with courtly tradition and principles. But Edward stuck to his guns. He was in love with Wallis Simpson, who was not allowed to become Queen because she had been divorced, and he had no intention of giving her up.

Fort Belvedere

During the crisis, played out against the backdrops of the House of Commons and the House of Windsor, Edward spent much of his time at Fort Belvedere, his beloved country residence near fashionable Sunningdale. Originally constructed by William, Duke of Cumberland, as a triangular belvedere tower in the 1730s, the building was later enlarged to become a miniature fortress for royal tea parties, the home of a royal collection of guns and for storing various family treasures. A battery of cannon was even installed, to be fired on royal birthdays by a resident bombardier. 'It was a child's idea of a fort', wrote Diana Cooper, a leading figure in royal circles and high society, 'the sentries, one thought, must be of tin'.

It was back in the 1920s, years before the crisis, that the Prince of Wales asked his father if he could use Fort Belvedere. He replied: 'What could you want that queer old place for? Those damn weekends I suppose'. Something of a playboy, Edward was a noted socialite who liked to entertain regularly and on a lavish scale. He was allowed to take up residence here, but in later years the house became much more than just a country retreat.

In the closing stages of the crisis, Edward asked his brothers to visit him at Fort Belvedere and witness his signature on the abdication document. It was signed at 12:45PM on Thursday December 10, 1936 in one of the King's private rooms. A few members of his secretarial staff were present and outside, on the Ascot road, a crowd gathered to see him leave the fort for the last time.

Happiest days

Long after he had given up the throne and gone into exile, Fort Belvedere still occupied his thoughts. In his memoirs, Edward wrote fondly of the house that 'laid hold of me in so many ways'. When he finally drove away from Fort Belvedere, it seemed to him like a symbol of all he was giving up. 'The Fort had been more than a home', he wrote, 'it had been a way of life for me… it was there that I passed the happiest days of my life'.

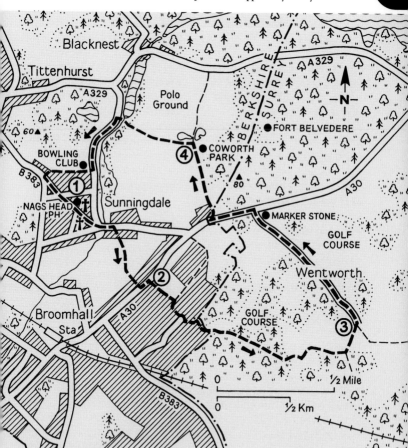

Walk 26 **Directions**

① From the **Nags Head** turn left and walk down the **High Street**, keeping the Anglican church on your right and the Baptist church on the left. Pass **Church Road** and continue along **Bedford Lane**. Cross a brook and turn right by some bungalows to follow a path cutting between hedgerows and fields. Look

Walk 26

for a sizeable house with shutters on the right, just before the **A30**. Bear left and walk along to a sign on the right for **Shrubs Hill Lane** and **Onslow Road**.

② Follow the leafy path to a junction by a panel fence and turn right by the bridleway/footpath sign. Curve left, make for a roundabout and swing left, looking for the footpath next to a house called **Highgate**. Follow it through the woodland and when you join a wider path on a bend, keep left. Skirt the golf course, cutting between trees and bracken, and when you emerge from the woodland, follow the path across the fairways, keeping left at a junction by a bunker. Veer left at the first fork, into the trees, and follow the path to a junction with a tarmac drive.

③ Turn left and pass through the **Wentworth Estate**, cutting between exclusive houses with secluded landscaped grounds and imposing entrances. On reaching the **A30**, turn left and follow the road west. Walk down to the Berkshire/Surrey border and bear sharp right to join a right of way. Follow the shaded woodland path between beech trees and exposed roots. Beyond the wood you reach the buildings of **Coworth Park**.

④ Draw level with a bridge, turn left and follow the well-defined footpath across a broad expanse of parkland, part of which is used as a polo ground, crossing a track on the far side. Enter woodland, turn left at the road and pass several houses. When you reach the speed restriction sign, bear right to join a byway by **Sunningdale Bowling Club**. Keep to a tarmac drive and continue ahead. Turn left at the road, swinging left after a few paces at the fork. Pass **Coworth Road** and return to the centre of **Sunningdale** village.

WHILE YOU'RE THERE ⓘ
Stroll through the **Wentworth Estate** on the Berkshire/Surrey border and you'll see that most houses have their own security. Some even boast their own monogrammed gates. General Pinochet was detained here at the end of the 1990s, making newspaper headlines for some months. It was back in the 1920s that Wentworth began to evolve into the community you see today. What had been a private country estate was sold off in separate lots and sizeable new houses began to spring up.

WHAT TO LOOK FOR ⓘ
On reaching the A30 from the Wentworth Estate, turn right for a few paces to see one of the entrances to **Fort Belvedere** on the north side of the road, while to the south of it, half hidden in the foliage, lies an old marker stone indicating that it is 22 miles (35.4km) from here to London's Hyde Park Corner. **Coworth Park**, originally the seat of the Earl of Derby, belongs to a Canadian millionaire, with part of the estate owned by the Brunei Government and run as a polo centre. The house is built in the style of a medieval Swiss farmhouse. To the east of Coworth Park lies Fort Belvedere, enclosed by thick woodland. To the north lie Virginia Water and Windsor Great Park (► Walk 27).

Windsor's Great Park

Royal footsteps on the Long Walk.

•DISTANCE•	5½ miles (8.8km)
•MINIMUM TIME•	2hrs 30min
•ASCENT / GRADIENT•	160ft (49m) ▲▲▲
•LEVEL OF DIFFICULTY•	🚶 🚶 🚶
•PATHS•	Park drives and rides, woodland paths and tracks
•LANDSCAPE•	Sprawling parkland of Windsor Great Park
•SUGGESTED MAP•	aqua3 OS Explorer 160 Windsor, Weybridge & Bracknell
•START / FINISH•	Grid reference: SU 947727
•DOG FRIENDLINESS•	Dogs under strict control or on lead
•PARKING•	Car park by Cranbourne Gate
•PUBLIC TOILETS•	None on route

BACKGROUND TO THE WALK

Walkers in East Berkshire who enjoy peaceful parkland, leafy paths and a sense of space in a noisy and cluttered world don't have to look very far to find what they want. Right on their doorstep is the opportunity to walk for miles and yet remain within the confines of Windsor Great Park, once part of a royal hunting ground and now, in effect, an enormous nature reserve covering thousands of acres, where many different animals – deer among them – roam freely and undisturbed amid the ancient trees.

Windsor Great Park stretches south from Windsor Castle for about 5 miles (8km), almost as far as Chobham Common in Surrey. Comprising about 4,800 acres (1,944ha) of wooded parkland and magnificent landscaped gardens, the general design and landscaping is largely the work of George III's uncle, the Duke of Cumberland, who was given the rangership of Windsor Great Park in recognition of his victory over the Jacobites at the Battle of Culloden in 1746.

One of the park's most striking features is the oak-lined Long Walk, running in a straight line between Windsor and the mighty equestrian statue of George III on Snow Hill, erected in 1831 and known as the Copper Horse. Many members of the Royal Family have followed the Long Walk over the years, among the most recent royals to do so, in front of gathering crowds and television cameras, was Sophie, Countess of Wessex, who travelled by car through the Great Park in 1999, on her way to St George's Chapel where she married Prince Edward.

Copper Horse

The statue of the Copper Horse offers one of the most photographed views in Britain – that of Windsor Castle. During the late 1950s, the exiled Duke of Windsor described the royal residence and its surroundings thus: 'there is one place... which hardly changes at all, and that is Windsor Castle. Here is a palace essentially English in character. I take pleasure in the way it broods, with an air of comfortable benevolence, down over the homely town of Windsor, while to the south spreads the spacious Great Park, with the Long Walk stretching three miles through the soft, green English landscape and the meadows of the Home Park to the south, refreshed by the waters of the slowly winding Thames'.

But it is not just royals and ramblers who have loved Windsor Great Park over the years. Writers have been captivated and inspired by it, too. Alexander Pope often rode here and was moved to write about the scenery, Jonathan Swift reported that Queen Anne was 'hunting the stag till four this afternoon', while Swift described the Long Walk as 'the finest avenue I ever saw'.

Walk 27 **Directions**

① From the car park, cross the **A332** to **Cranbourne Gate** and enter the park. Follow the drive alongside trees planted over the years to commemorate Queen Victoria's Golden Jubilee in 1887 and Edward VII's coronation in 1902. Over to the left are distant views of Windsor Castle. Turn right at the first crossroads, signposted

'Cumberland Lodge', and follow the drive to the next junction by two ponds where swans are often seen.

② Keep left here, signposted 'The Village'. Pass the **Post Office and General Store**, walk between a spacious green and a playing field and then turn right to join **Queen Anne's Ride**. Look back for another view of Windsor Castle, framed by the houses of The Village. Pass alongside **Poets Lawn** and follow

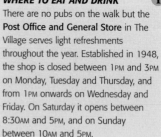

Walk 27

WHILE YOU'RE THERE ⓘ

Visit **Savill Gardens**, comprising 35 acres (14ha) of unspoilt woodland, herbaceous borders, azaleas, magnolias and rhododendrons. The garden was created by Sir Eric Savill, Deputy Ranger of the Great Park, between 1932 and 1949. Have a look at **The Village**, which was designed in the 1930s whilst the Duke and Duchess of York lived at Royal Lodge. Some of the later houses, which are occupied by estate workers, were built with bricks brought in from London bomb sites. Take a break on **Snow Hill** and enjoy the fine views of Windsor Castle and the Great Park. This is one of the highest points in the park and it was here on June 6, 1977 that the Queen lit a huge bonfire to mark her Silver Jubilee.

the ride to a tarmac drive. Turn left, keep left at the fork, then left again after a few paces at a crossroads.

③ **Poets Lawn** is now on your left. Continue ahead at the next intersection and then turn right to follow a broad, hedge-lined footpath. Ahead lies **Royal Lodge** and to the left of it is the famous **Copper Horse statue**. Take the next grassy ride on the left and head for a deer gate. Keep ahead towards the statue and when you draw level with it, bear left. The figure of George III points the way. Follow the woodland path and merge with a clear track running down to a drive. Pass through the automatic gate and keep right at the immediate fork.

④ Walk along to **Queen Anne's Ride**, which crosses the drive just before a house. On the left is the **millstone**. Bear right here and follow the ride to **Russel's Pond**. Veer away from the ride at this point and keep alongside the pond and fence. Walk ahead between fields and make for woodland. Drop down to the road at **Ranger's Gate**. Cross over at the lights and take the tarmac drive.

WHERE TO EAT AND DRINK ⓘ

There are no pubs on the walk but the **Post Office and General Store** in The Village serves light refreshments throughout the year. Established in 1948, the shop is closed between 1PM and 3PM on Monday, Tuesday and Thursday, and from 1PM onwards on Wednesday and Friday. On Saturday it opens between 8:30AM and 5PM, and on Sunday between 10AM and 5PM.

⑤ Veer half left about 100yds (91m) before some white gates and follow a path across the grass and alongside trees. Follow it up the slope and through the wood. Keep to the sandy track and at the point where it bends left, go straight on along a path between trees. As it reaches a gate, turn left and keep alongside a fence. The path can be rather overgrown in places in summer. Follow the fence to a drive and on the right is the outline of **Cranbourne Tower**. Bear left and return to the car park.

WHAT TO LOOK FOR ⓘ

On Queen Anne's Ride stands a **millstone** which was unveiled to commemorate the planting of the first of 1,000 trees here, marking 1,000 years of the office of High Sheriff of Windsor Great Park. The trees were planted by the Duke of Edinburgh, Ranger of Windsor Great Park, on 23 November 1992. The millstone was carved at Stanage Edge in Derbyshire. Almost at the end of the walk is **Cranbourne Tower**, part of a lodge visited by Samuel Pepys in 1665 and where Queen Victoria took tea. Pepys would have probably seen the lodge while out riding. During the 1800s, parts of the building which were structurally dangerous were removed, leaving only the tower.

21/11/2010   *with Ann*
pleasant week

Danger Lurked at Dusk in Maidenhead Thicket

A pretty walk through extensive woodland, once the haunt of highwaymen.

•DISTANCE•	3½ miles (5.7km)
•MINIMUM TIME•	1hr 30min
•ASCENT / GRADIENT•	82ft (25m)
•LEVEL OF DIFFICULTY•	
•PATHS•	Field and woodland paths, some road walking, 2 stiles
•LANDSCAPE•	Mixture of farmland and woodland to west of Maidenhead
•SUGGESTED MAP•	aqua3 OS Explorers 160 Windsor, Weybridge & Bracknell; 172 Chiltern Hills East
•START / FINISH•	Grid reference: SU 838800 (on Explorer 172)
•DOG FRIENDLINESS•	On lead across farmland and under control in woodland
•PARKING•	By green in village of Littlewick Green
•PUBLIC TOILETS•	None on route

BACKGROUND TO THE WALK

Maidenhead Thicket is one of those delightful places that you might frequently pass by in the car without even realising it's there. From the road, only a curtain of trees is visible, but step into Maidenhead Thicket and at once you are in a tranquil world of dense woodland and sunny glades. Lime trees, oaks and horse chestnuts bring colour and life to the well-used paths and tracks, and for a few short weeks every year the ground is covered with violets and hazy blue carpets of bluebells.

Haunt of Highwaymen

Maidenhead Thicket consists of 368 acres (149ha) of woodland and glades. These days it is National Trust land, but it is probably best known as a notorious haunt of highwaymen. The trees and bushes lining the Great West Road would have given these 18th-century muggers perfect cover as they lay in wait for passing stage coaches.

The nearby town of Maidenhead once boasted scores of inns which prospered on the vulnerability of coach passengers. Most opted to stay in the town overnight rather than risk driving through the dreaded thicket at dusk. It is also claimed that the highwaymen who lurked under the trees preferred the coaches entering the town from the west. Those approaching from the east had already been robbed by the highwaymen of Hounslow Heath.

Dangerous Times

Claude Duval (1643–70), one of the best-known highwaymen, preyed upon travellers in this area. According to a handbook on Berkshire, Buckinghamshire and Oxfordshire, published in 1860, 'in the reign of Elizabeth, the vicar of Hurley, who served the cure of Maidenhead, was allowed an extra salary to atone for the danger of passing the thicket'. Dick Turpin (1705–39) travelled this way too, waiting in the shadows to ambush any passing coaches. From here he galloped to his aunt's cottage at nearby Sonning where he stabled his horse, Black Bess, before going into hiding in Oxfordshire until the dust settled.

Black Mask

Jackson's *Oxford Journal* for 1 November 1755 tells of a typical hold-up: 'Last Tuesday about 12:00 at noon, the Oxford machine (the stage coach from London), in which were three gentlemen, was stopped by a single highwayman, well mounted, with a black mask, in Maidenhead Thicket. Upon demanding their money, the passengers gave him about 12 guineas. He then demanded their watches, which two of the gentlemen delivered, but one of them desiring he would return the seal, on which was his coat of arms. The highwayman, observing that the watch was only pinchbeck, said it would be of little service to him and returned it. He then made off into the thicket'.

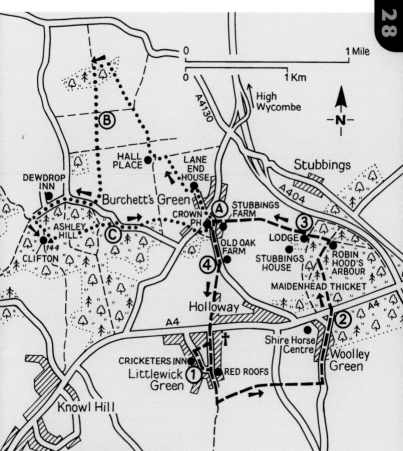

Walk 28 Directions

① Head for the south east corner of the green in the centre of **Littlewick Green**, turn right into **School Lane** and follow it to the woodland edge. Emerging from the trees, bear left to join a made-up, tarmac track

running across the fields. There are good views to the south along here. Cross a road leading to a business park and continue over farmland to the next road. Turn left, pass an assortment of houses lining the route and walk almost to the **A4**, keeping right at the junction just before it.

Walk 28

② Cross over and enter **Maidenhead Thicket**, following the path between trees and clearings. On reaching a muddy bridleway, veer right and follow the main route along to the next junction. This represents the site of **Robin Hood's Arbour**. Turn left here and follow the hard path to reach the lodge to **Stubbings House**.

③ Cross two stiles to the right of it and then follow the path out across the fields. The footpath graduates to a track before arriving at the buildings of **Stubbings Farm**. On reaching the road at **Burchett's Green**, turn left and pass some houses, one of which has a white weatherboarded tower. Follow the lane and veer half right just beyond the entrance to **Old Oak Farm**.

④ Follow the path between hedgerows and trees and further on it runs alongside houses and bungalows. Along this stretch the path broadens to a track. The sound of traffic on the **A4** gradually

becomes audible. At the junction go straight over into **Jubilee Road** and follow it towards the cricket ground at **Littlewick Green**. On reaching the edge of the green, bear right to join a waymarked footpath running alongside the ground and past the front of Littlewick Green cricket club. At the road turn left, passing the **Cricketers Inn**. Alternatively, follow the road round the eastern edge of the green to the start.

On to Hall Place

Cross picturesque grounds to reach woodland on the slopes of Ashley Hill.
See map and information panel for Walk 28

•**DISTANCE**•	7½ miles (12.1km)
•**MINIMUM TIME**•	3hrs
•**ASCENT / GRADIENT**•	262ft (80m) ▲▲▲
•**LEVEL OF DIFFICULTY**•	狀 狀 狀

Walk 29 Directions
(Walk 28 option)

At Point Ⓐ, turn right at the road and keep the **Crown** on the left. Cross over into **Hall Place Lane**, keeping left at the entrance to **Lane End House**. Take the path to a gate and cross the field to an avenue of trees. Head towards **Hall Place** and swing right in front of the house.

Hall Place is Georgian and until the Second World War was owned by the Clayton East family. Sold to the Ministry of Agriculture, the house and part of the estate were acquired by Berkshire County Council in 1949 for the Berkshire Institute of Agriculture, later the Berkshire College of Agriculture.

Follow the drive to reach the vet's and veer half left just beyond it at the waymark. Once clear of the enclosures, pass between trees and bushes to a crossroads. Keep left at the fork just beyond it and follow the clear track towards woodland. Make for a galvanised gate and take the path to the far end of the wood, swinging left to follow the fence. On reaching a pair of gates and a waymark, turn left and cut back through the wood. Make for

another gate and then continue ahead between fields, towards the tree-clad slopes of **Ashley Hill**.

At Point Ⓑ, cross two tracks and go through a gate, crossing the field to a gate. Follow the waymarked path through a belt of trees to the next gate and continue along the field edge. Pass a house and cross a stile out to the road. Turn right and follow the woodland perimeter. Go straight ahead at the bend, passing the turning to the **Dewdrop Inn.** Continue ahead at a 'private' sign and follow the path to a waymarked junction. Bear left here, up through the trees. Pass over a cross track and keep left at the fork. Ahead is the entrance to **Clifton**, an isolated house. Turn left here and follow the drive down through the woods. As it eventually sweeps to the right, go straight on to the road, Point Ⓒ.

Keep right and, when the road begins to curve to the right, look for a footpath branching left through the trees. Cross two stiles and skirt a fence and stream. Follow the path over a track by a gate and keep ahead towards houses. Cross two stiles to the road and look for two paths opposite. Keep left and cut through the wood to Furze Cottage. Turn right and head for **Old Oak Farm** at Point ④ on Walk 28.

Walk 30

Stanley Spencer's Cookham

A spectacular stretch of the Thames Path to Bourne End, returning by train.

•**DISTANCE**•	7 miles (11.3km)
•**MINIMUM TIME**•	3hrs
•**ASCENT / GRADIENT**•	Negligible
•**LEVEL OF DIFFICULTY**•	
•**PATHS**	Pavements, riverside promenade, Thames Path, 1 stile
•**LANDSCAPE**•	Riverside, fields and meadows
•**SUGGESTED MAP**•	aqua3 OS Explorer 172 Chiltern Hills East
•**START / FINISH**•	Grid reference: SU 887807
•**DOG FRIENDLINESS**•	On lead in Maidenhead, Cookham and Bourne End
•**PARKING**•	Maidenhead Station
•**PUBLIC TOILETS**•	Maidenhead Station

Walk 30 Directions

From the car park walk down to the clock tower, erected to mark Queen Victoria's diamond jubilee in 1897. Cross the road at the lights and bear right into **Queen Street**, by the **Bell** pub. Veer right into **York Road** and pass the football club. Walk down to the mini-roundabout and turn left into **Forlease Road**. Head for the next junction and turn right into **Moorbridge Road**.

WHERE TO EAT AND DRINK ⓘ

Maidenhead and Cookham offer a good choice of pubs and eating places. You might like to stop off at Jenner's Cafe near Boulter's Lock. Hot food is served all day, including full breakfast, and there are hot and cold drinks and ice cream. If you have to wait for the train back to Maidenhead, call into the Firefly pub next door to Bourne End Station.

Walk along to the underpass and veer right on the far side, following **Bridge Road** towards **Maidenhead Bridge**. Pass some almshouses and a sign for the Thames before reaching the bridge. Cross the bridge almost to the opposite bank and look downstream to the right. Straddling the river is Brunel's famous railway bridge. Return to the Maidenhead side of the river and bear right into **Ray Mead Road**. Make for **Boulter's Lock** and continue to the point where the road and the Thames Path part company. Follow the tow path. The view over to the Buckinghamshire bank is dominated by the beautiful hanging beech woods of the Cliveden estate.

Soon the sound of traffic fades as the walk turns its back on Maidenhead, following the Thames upstream towards **Cookham**. There is a brief glimpse of **Cliveden**, seen high above the beeches.

Eventually the path swings away from the riverbank and cuts through woodland to reach a stile. Cross over and veer slightly left, keeping to the right of a house. Head for a tarmac drive and turn left opposite **Sol Mill**. Walk along to the junction, bear right and follow the road into **Cookham**.

The village will forever be associated with the artist Stanley Spencer who died in 1959. Spencer was a controversial eccentric figure and even now, more than 40 years after his death, his work is the subject of speculation and debate. He was born in Cookham High Street in 1891 and spent most of his life in the village. The former Methodist chapel on the corner of the High Street and the A4094 is now a gallery devoted to his work.

WHAT TO LOOK FOR

Perched on cliffs above the Thames is **Cliveden**, an Italianate mansion built for the Duke of Sutherland in 1850–1. The house was once the home of the Astor family. During the early 1960s, Cliveden, together with the riverside dwellings below it, became the focus of national attention when the Profumo scandal was played out here, resulting in lurid newspaper headlines and frenzied gossip in society circles. Its final outcome was the resignation of a prominent Cabinet minister, John Profumo, after his affair with a very young Christine Keeler became public.

It was to this chapel that Mrs Spencer marched young Stanley and her eight other children every Sunday. Officially opened in 1962, the gallery exhibits many of Spencer's paintings, including *The Last Supper*, painted in 1920, and the view of *Cookham from Englefield*, completed in 1948. There is also an extensive collection of drawings, including much of his early work. *The Fairy on the Waterlily Leaf* and *Roy*, from 1909 and 1906 respectively, are here.

In addition to examples of Spencer's highly individual style, there is a permanent collection at Cookham of his letters, documents and notes, together with the pram

in which Spencer wheeled his paints and brushes when painting landscapes. He was often seen pushing it around the village.

Cookham played a key role in Spencer's work, forming the setting for many biblical and figure paintings, as well as landscapes. Cookham Moor, the parish church and the High Street are all shown on canvas. The Sandham Memorial Chapel at Burghclere south of Newbury contains murals inspired by Spencer's experiences in the First World War.

Pass the **Stanley Spencer Gallery** and continue along the road, passing the **Tarry Stone**. Veer left at the entrance to the church, pass the memorial stone to Spencer, keep to the left of **Holy Trinity** and walk through the churchyard to rejoin the **Thames Path**. Swing left and pass **Cookham Reach Sailing Club**. Cross the meadow and keep close to the water's edge. Up ahead is Bourne End railway bridge.

Pass beneath the bridge and turn immediately left, go up the steps and cross the footbridge to the Buckinghamshire bank. Once over the bridge, turn right and pass a house called **The Haven**. Keep left at this point and follow the drive alongside a high brick wall to the road. Turn left and walk along to the station at **Bourne End** to catch the train back to Maidenhead.

WHILE YOU'RE THERE

On reaching the Thames, look downstream for a good view of Brunel's splendid railway bridge, which has the widest and flattest brick arches in the world. J M W Turner made it the subject of his famous painting: *Rain, Steam and Speed* (1844).

Colourful Wargrave

Leave bustling Wargrave and head for peaceful Bowsey Hill.

•DISTANCE•	6 miles (9.7km)
•MINIMUM TIME•	2hrs 15min
•ASCENT / GRADIENT•	248ft (76m) ▲▲▲
•LEVEL OF DIFFICULTY•	🚶 🚶 🚶
•PATHS•	Stretches of road, field and woodland paths, 13 stiles
•LANDSCAPE•	High ground on upper slopes of Thames Valley, dense woodland and peaceful glades
•SUGGESTED MAP•	aqua3 OS Explorer 171 Chiltern Hills West
•START / FINISH•	Grid reference: SU 786785
•DOG FRIENDLINESS•	On lead near livestock and where requested by signs
•PARKING•	Public car park in School Lane, just off A321
•PUBLIC TOILETS•	At car park

BACKGROUND TO THE WALK

The riverside village of Wargrave is usually quiet during the week, but often busy with visitors and boating enthusiasts at the weekends, particularly in the summer. It is sometimes mistakenly believed that the village has a connection with military cemeteries. That couldn't be further from the truth – its name actually means 'grove by the weirs'.

The village is distinctly Edwardian in appearance but its origins date back many centuries. When Edith, the wife of Edward the Confessor, held the manor in the 11th century, it was known as Weregrave. The church among the trees dates from the First World War, replacing an earlier building that, except for the Norman tower, was destroyed by fire on Whit Sunday, 1914. It is believed that the fire was the work of a militant wing of the Suffragettes – angry because the vicar would not withdraw the word 'obey' from the marriage service. However, this claim was never proved. Madame Tussaud's daughter-in-law is buried in the churchyard.

Colourful Residents

Thomas Day, the 18th-century idealist, was a resident of Wargrave. He wrote *Sandford and Merton* (1783–9), the story of two boys – one rich, the other poor. Day was an eccentric character but a genial man, nonetheless. He supported the abolition of slavery and the protection of animals from cruelty. He believed, too, that animals responded to kindness and gentleness. However, this proved to be his undoing. One day in 1789, in an attempt to demonstrate his conviction, he mounted an unbroken horse and was subsequently thrown off and killed.

Wargrave seems to have produced more than its fair share of colourful characters over the centuries. One of them was Zachary Allnutt who lived for more than 100 years at Lavender Cottage on the Henley road. Allnutt was a well-known local lavender grower in the 19th century. He had 40 acres (16ha) of it and the air around Wargrave at that time must have been very fragrant.

Another eccentric local figure was the 18th-century Irish peer, the Earl of Barrymore. He built a theatre close to his Wargrave home and engaged the services of a famous Covent

Garden clown known as Delphini. The opening night in 1791 was a sensation, with the cream of theatrical society in attendance. The Earl died suddenly in 1793, and by that time he had frittered away over £¼ million on the theatre, as well as various other sporting pleasures. There is a final, rather sordid, footnote to this story. The Earl was buried at Wargrave church on a Sunday so as to prevent his creditors seizing his body and holding it until his debts had been settled!

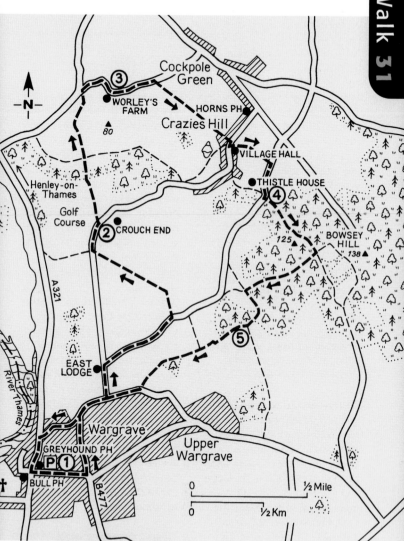

Walk 31 **Directions**

① Turn left and walk along **School Lane**, the B477. On the first bend, bear left into **Dark Lane**, head up the hill and turn right at the T-junction. Follow the road and turn left at the sign for Crazies Hill. Bear right by **East Lodge**, follow the lane to a bend and bear left over a stile to join a waymarked path.

Walk 31

Keep alongside the fence, and then strike out across the fields towards trees. Cross a stile and turn right at the road, veering left opposite a private house, **Crouch End**.

② Keep close to the left boundary of the field and look for a stile in the bottom corner. Descend steeply to two stiles and a bridleway beyond. Cross a stile almost opposite and climb the hillside. Look for a stile further up the slope and keep ahead on the higher ground, following the path alongside the fence. Descend to a kissing gate at the road and turn immediately right. Head uphill and pass **Worley's Farm**.

WHAT TO LOOK FOR

The pretty hamlet of **Crazies Hill** lies on the upper slopes of the valley. There is a rather charming story behind its name. Apparently, buttercups were once commonplace in this area and 'crazies' is a rustic country name for buttercups. Look out for the entrance to **Thistle House**. In the 1960s this was the home of David Greig, a butcher who began a supermarket chain. His emblem was the thistle and the house was used as a training college for a while.

---

③ Take the next waymarked path on the right, just before a row of trees, and aim a little to the left as you cross the field, lining up with a large white house in the distance. Head towards a stile in the hedge and maintain the same direction, keeping to the left of the house. Look for a stile and follow an enclosed path to the road. Turn right, then left beside the village hall and, after a few paces, bear left by the old **Old Clubhouse**. Follow the path by a paddock to a stile by the road. Bear right, past the entrance to **Thistle House** and a bridleway into trees on the right.

WHILE YOU'RE THERE

As you approach Crazies Hill look across the fields towards nearby **Cockpole Green**. It is believed there was once a cockpit here where cock fighting took place. Along the road to Remenham Hill, at Upper Culham Farm, was a RAF airfield. During the Second World War the residents of this area would have become used to the sound of droning aircraft overhead.

---

④ Continue for several paces to a stile on the left. Join a woodland path and look out for white arrows on the tree trunks, eventually reaching a waymarked junction. Turn right here, avoid a path on the right and keep going to the next waymarked junction, on the edge of the wood. Fields are visible here. Bear left and walk down to a flight of steps and a footbridge. Make for the woodland perimeter and turn right along the field edge.

⑤ Cross a bridleway via two stiles and continue ahead along the woodland edge. Look for a hedge gap on the right, cross into the adjoining field and maintain the same direction. Make for a kissing gate and a footbridge in the field corner and continue ahead to a wrought iron kissing gate. Follow the path across the next field, heading towards trees. Make for a kissing gate leading out to the road and turn right. Follow it down to the **A321**, turn left and walk along to **School Lane**.

WHERE TO EAT AND DRINK

There are several pubs in Wargrave – among them the **Bull**, the **Greyhound** and the **White Hart**. Alternatively, if you want to stop midway round the walk, try the **Horns** at Crazies Hill. This popular timber-framed pub has a range of filled baguettes and daily-changing menus.

A World of Water and Wildlife at Dinton Pastures

This fascinating walk mostly stays within the boundaries of a popular country park, visiting six different lakes along the way.

•**DISTANCE**•	3 miles (4.8km)
•**MINIMUM TIME**•	1hr 30min
•**ASCENT / GRADIENT**•	Negligible
•**LEVEL OF DIFFICULTY**•	
•**PATHS**•	Lakeside and riverside paths, some road walking, no stiles
•**LANDSCAPE**•	Extensive lakeland
•**SUGGESTED MAP**•	aqua3 OS Explorer 159 Reading, Wokingham & Pangbourne
•**START / FINISH**•	Grid reference: SU 7847186
•**DOG FRIENDLINESS**•	Dogs under control and on lead where requested
•**PARKING**•	Large car park at Dinton Pastures
•**PUBLIC TOILETS**•	Dinton Pastures

BACKGROUND TO THE WALK

Dinton Pastures Country Park describes itself as a mosaic of rivers, meadows, lakes and woodland. The lakes were once gravel workings that were flooded to form the focal point of this attractive recreational area. Paths and self-guided trails enable visitors to explore this tranquil world of water and wildlife at will and, as you explore the park on foot, spare a thought to work out how it all began.

The Early Days

The park's river meadows were once farmed by Anglo Saxons who called the area Whistley – 'wisc' meaning marshy meadow and 'lei', a wooded glade or clearing. The River Loddon was also used as part of the same process, farmed for its rich supply of eels, caught in willow traps for the monks of Abingdon Abbey. Traps were still in regular use as late as the 1930s.

By the beginning of the 17th century, much of the area formed part of Windsor Forest, where the Monarch and his courtiers indulged in hunting for pleasure. It was the courtiers who built some of the region's grandest houses, including High Chimneys, which was handy for Windsor Castle, the royal powerhouse. High Chimneys' farmhouse, which later became the Tea Cosy café, dates back to 1904. During the mid-1920s it was occupied by a farmer who named the farm after his home village of Dinton, near Aylesbury.

Dinton Pastures forms part of the Loddon's flood plain and is a rich source of gravel, which has been extracted here for more than 100 years. There was an extensive extraction programme here during the late 1960s and right through the 1970s. Much of the material was used to construct the M4 and the A329(M), connecting Reading and Wokingham.

Recreational Area

Comprising about 230 acres (93ha) and officially opened to the public in 1979, Dinton Pastures attracts many visitors who come here to walk, fish, picnic and indulge in birdwatching – a welcome green space on Reading's doorstep. The largest of the lakes at

Dinton Pastures is Black Swan. The Emm Brook once flowed where the lake is now situated. It was later diverted and the oaks which you can see on the island in the lake were once on the banks of the old stream.

All the lakes draw a variety of wetland birds such as swans, geese, coots and moorhens. The park's rarest birds are bitterns – less than 20 pairs breed in Britain annually. Several fly here in winter and in spring migrants such as nightingales also make the journey from Africa to nest at Dinton Pastures. The park offers all sorts of surprises – you may spot a weasel or a stoat, catch sight of a mink in the Loddon, or identify one of 18 species of dragonfly in the lakes and rivers.

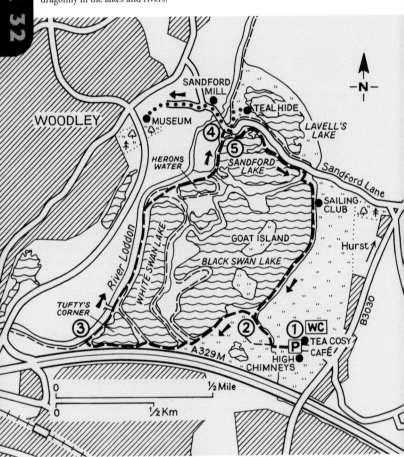

Walk 32 **Directions**

① With the **Tea Cosy** café and Countryside Service office on the right and **High Chimneys** behind you, cross the car park to the large map of the site. Follow the wide path and keep right at the fork by the 'wildlife trails' sign. Pass an enclosed play area on the left, keep the **Emm Brook** on the right and enjoy the tantalizing glimpses of **Black Swan Lake** up ahead.

② Swing left on reaching the water and follow the path alongside the lake. When it veers right, turn left

Walk 32

across a bridge to a sign for Tufty's Corner. Bear right here and keep left at the fork after a few paces. Follow the path beside **White Swan Lake** to a waymark post by a patch of grass and a flight of steps. Avoid the steps but take the left-hand path and follow it to the lake known as **Tufty's Corner**. On reaching a junction by a bridge, turn right and keep the **River Loddon** on your left.

③ Walk along to the next bridge. Don't cross it; instead continue on the riverside path. White Swan Lake lies over to the right, glimpsed at intervals between the trees. Further on, the path curves to the right, in line with the river, before reaching a sign 'private fishing – members only'. Join a track on the right here and bear left. Pass alongside **Herons Water** to a sign 'Sandford Lake, Black Swan Lake and Lavell's Lake – Conservation Area'. Turn left and keep **Sandford Lake** on the right. When the path curves right, go out to the road.

④ To visit the **Berkshire Museum of Aviation**, bear left and pass **Sandford Mill**. Take the road signposted 'No Through Road' on the left, pass several cottages and continue ahead when the road dwindles to a path. The museum is on the left. Retrace your steps to Sandford Mill and keep walking ahead to a footpath and kissing gate on the left. Keep left at the first fork, then right at the second and head for the **Teal hide**. Return to the road, cross over and return to the lakeside path.

WHAT TO LOOK FOR ℹ
Sandford Mill, built in 1772, was in use until the mid-1950s and in 1994 it was converted into a private property. A mill was originally recorded on this site in the Domesday Book. With the trees surrounding it and its picturesque white weatherboarded façade, it creates a pretty picture in this corner of the park.

⑤ Continue with **Sandford Lake** on your right. On reaching a sign 'Sandford Lake – wildlife area – dogs under control' veer left over a bridge and turn left. **Black Swan Sailing Club** can be seen on the left. Continue on the broad path and look out across the lake to **Goat Island**, noted for its population of goats. On reaching the picnic area overlooking **Black Swan Lake**, turn left and retrace your steps back to the main car park.

WHILE YOU'RE THERE ℹ
Visit the **Teal Hide** at Lavell's Lake, overlooking the wader scrapes. See if you can spot wading birds from here – look out for the green sandpiper and redshank, ducks, swans, kingfishers and the occasional bittern. This site is for serious ornithologists. Not long ago this corner of the park was a meadow grazed by cattle or cut for hay, though the landscape changed dramatically at the time of gravel extraction. Take time to visit the **Berkshire Museum of Aviation**, just off the main route of the walk. The museum is dedicated to the contribution the county has made to flying. A Second World War hangar has been moved here from Woodley and there are various aircraft representing Berkshire's aviation history from the last 60 years or so.

Walk 33

Wokingham to the Country

Discover a typical market town before heading for open countryside.

•DISTANCE•	6½ miles (10.4km)
•MINIMUM TIME•	2hrs 45min
•ASCENT / GRADIENT•	Negligible
•LEVEL OF DIFFICULTY•	
•PATHS•	Streets, forest and field paths, tracks, 1 stile
•LANDSCAPE•	Town streets and well-wooded countryside
•SUGGESTED MAP•	aqua3 OS Explorer 159 Reading, Wokingham & Pangbourne
•START / FINISH•	Grid reference: SX 106836
•DOG FRIENDLINESS•	Under control in woodland, on lead by paddocks
•PARKING•	Public car parks in Rose Street and Denmark Street
•PUBLIC TOILETS•	Rose Street and Denmark Street

BACKGROUND TO THE WALK

A classic market town, Wokingham is full of hidden corners and picturesque old buildings. Before starting this walk, get hold of a good street map and an informative booklet on the town and head off in search of the real Wokingham.

Founded in the 13th century by the Norman-French Bishop Roger le Poore, the town was granted a charter by Queen Elizabeth in 1583. Until the 19th century Wokingham developed at a slow pace, but in recent years it has grown enormously, its rapid expansion influenced by its close proximity to London and the M4.

At the heart of Wokingham, in its Market Place, stands the impressive Town Hall. The present building dates back to 1860, and was designed in the Gothic revival style. Originally, the Town Hall was a police station, a courtroom and a gaol. If you stand outside and look closely, you can spot 'County Police Station' inscribed in stone near the top of the building.

Just a stone's throw from the Town Hall lies Rose Street, one of Wokingham's hidden treasures and the finest example in Berkshire of a medieval 'enclosed' street. Founded by the Dean of Salisbury in the early 13th century, Rose Street is wide at one end and narrow at the other. At the far end stands All Saints Church, originally a small Saxon chapel that was enlarged in the 12th century and dedicated to All Saints by the Bishop of Salisbury in about 1193. James 'Sooty' Seaward lived in Rose Street and was the inspiration for Tom the chimney sweep, the central character in Charles Kingsley's classic *The Water Babies* (1863).

At the far end of Broad Street and dating back to the mid-16th century is the Tudor House, one of Wokingham's most historic and attractive buildings. The front was partly altered in the early 20th century by incorporating timbers from a nearby dismantled mansion. Until the end of the First World War, the building housed a school. Next to the Tudor House is Wokingham Police Station, built in 1904 to the design of the county architect. The distinctive pagoda-style tower complements the building's striking chimneys.

Running south west from the Market Place is Denmark Street, a street that still evokes memories of old Wokingham. Many of the houses here were built in the 15th, 16th and 17th centuries. Until 1835 numbers 22 and 24 were part of the workhouse, later rebuilt elsewhere in the town. The Duke's Head pub at the bottom of the street was originally three cottages with a pond at the back used for tanning hides.

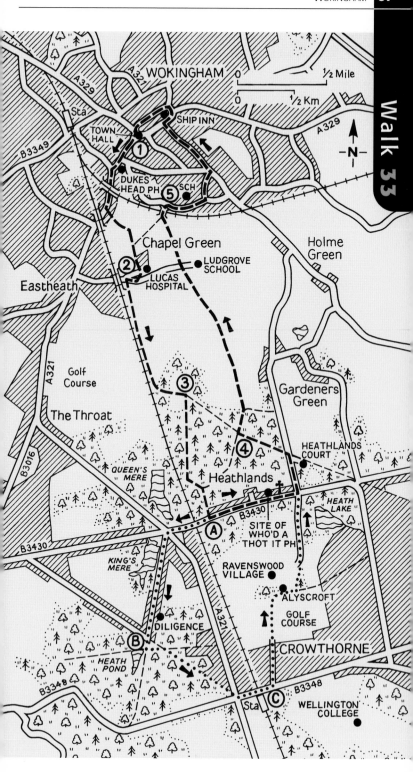

W a l k 3 3

Walk 33 Directions

① With the **Town Hall** on your right, walk down **Denmark Street**. Pass the Wokingham Memorial Clinic and keep right at the **Dukes Head**. Walk to the roundabout, cross **Kendrick Close** and follow **Finchampstead Road**. Pass under the railway and take the footpath on the left at the next roundabout. Head for a gate, veer right by some loose boxes and follow a fenced track. Make for a line of houses and continue to **Lucas Hospital**.

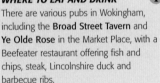

> **WHAT TO LOOK FOR**
>
> **Ludgrove School** is one of Berkshire's more famous preparatory schools. It achieved fame during the 1990s when the royal princes, William and Harry, attended the school.

② Look for a stile here and head diagonally right across the paddock to a wrought iron gate and a tarmac drive leading to **Ludgrove School**. Turn right, pass some white gateposts and bear left just beyond them at a pair of galvanised gates. Begin a lengthy stretch of track walking, keeping the railway line on your right. Eventually pass an old wartime **Nissen hut** and a cottage on the right. Continue for about 80yds (73m) and then turn right by some wooden posts.

③ Follow the track between plantations, avoid the path ahead at the left-hand bend and keep right at the next fork. Make for the road and turn left. Pass **Kingsbridge Cottages** and **Grove Close** before reaching the site of a former pub the Who'd a Thot It. Continue along the road to **St Sebastian's Church**, and turn left into **Heathlands Road**. Pass the entrance

to **Heathlands Court** and swing left just beyond it to join a byway by a sign for Bramshill Forest.

> **WHERE TO EAT AND DRINK**
>
> There are various pubs in Wokingham, including the **Broad Street Tavern** and **Ye Olde Rose** in the Market Place, with a Beefeater restaurant offering fish and chips, steak, Lincolnshire duck and barbecue ribs.

④ Swing right at the next waymarked junction and when the path bends right, go through a deer gate and carry on across market gardens. Continue between fences and fields and follow the path to the left of an entrance to **Ludgrove School**. Cut between laurel bushes and holly trees, cross a drive leading to the school and continue towards Wokingham. Keep ahead to a railway footbridge and veer right on the far side, following **Gypsy Lane**.

⑤ Pass **Southfields School**, cross **Erica Drive** and continue to the next main junction. Cross **Murdoch Road** and follow **Easthampstead Road** towards the town centre. Bear right at the T-junction and walk along to the Ship Inn. Keep left here, following **Wiltshire Road**, and turn left into **Rose Street**. Follow it back to the **Market Place**.

> **WHILE YOU'RE THERE**
>
> Enjoy the peace and quiet of **Bramshill Forest** around Nine Mile Ride (the B3430), the route of an old forest ride through what was Windsor Forest. On the left, just before St Sebastian's Church, is the site of a pub, the Who'd a Thot It, now closed. It's said that the 1st Duke of Wellington and his party stumbled on the inn quite by chance one day after hunting in the forest. Suitably refreshed, the Duke was heard to comment 'who would have thought it?'

Wellington at Crowthorne

Skirt the playing fields of an historic public school on this longer walk.
See map and information panel for Walk 33

·DISTANCE·	9½ miles (15.3km)
·MINIMUM TIME·	4hrs 30min
·ASCENT / GRADIENT·	Negligible
·LEVEL OF DIFFICULTY·	

Walk 34 Directions (Walk 33 option)

On reaching **Nine Mile Ride**, the B3430, between Points ③ and ④ on Walk 33, turn right at Point Ⓐ, cross the railway bridge and walk down to the roundabout. Cross **Lower Wokingham Road** and turn into **Hollybush Ride**. King's Mere can be seen on the right. Pass a house called **Diligence** on the left and continue ahead at an intersection of tracks.

This is part of Finchampstead Ridges, 60 acres (24ha) of lovely woodland, including a heather ridge and an extensive network of paths that are cared for by the National Trust. The area has much to interest the naturalist and ornithologist, with spotted flycatchers and siskins among the many species to be found here. If time allows, you may like to take a stroll and explore the attractive scenery.

At Point Ⓑ, with **Heath Pond** on the right, turn left at the next track junction and follow the byway, keeping right at the gates to a property called **Heritage**. Follow the track to a roundabout and take the second exit for Crowthorne. On the right are the playing fields of **Wellington College**.

One of Britain's most famous public schools, Wellington College dates back to the mid-19th century when it was founded as a memorial to the Duke of Wellington, following his victory at Waterloo in 1815. When it first opened, it was a school for the orphans of army officers. The railway station was originally known as Wellington College Station but changed its name after the First World War when Crowthorne began to expand.

Pass the railway station and a line of shops before turning left into **Ravenswood Avenue**, at Point Ⓒ. Walk along to the **East Berkshire Golf Club**, established in 1904, and follow the drive as it runs across the fairways. Look for a footpath sign and continue with the course now on your right. Pass a house called **Alyscroft** and take the next left footpath, following it along the woodland edge. Join a tarmac drive and pass alongside the buildings of **Ravenswood Village**, a community providing care for children with learning difficulties. Head for **Nine Mile Ride**, crossing over into **Heathlands Road**. Rejoin Walk 33 at Point ④ and follow the route back to the centre of Wokingham.

Walk 35

Finchampstead and Word of a Royal Bride

Enjoy a very pleasant country walk where kings and princes once hunted.

•DISTANCE•	5 miles (8km)
•MINIMUM TIME•	2hrs
•ASCENT / GRADIENT•	Negligible
•LEVEL OF DIFFICULTY•	
•PATHS•	Mainly field paths and tracks, 5 stiles
•LANDSCAPE•	Classic farmland on northern side of Blackwater Valley
•SUGGESTED MAP•	aqua3 OS Explorer 159 Reading, Wokingham & Pangbourne
•START / FINISH•	Grid reference: SU 793638
•DOG FRIENDLINESS•	On lead where there is livestock
•PARKING•	In vicinity of Finchampstead church and Queen's Oak
•PUBLIC TOILETS•	None on route

Walk 35 Directions

From the **Queen's Oak** turn right towards the church, following the footpath sign. Keep right as the lane forks and soon dwindles to a stony track, descending through a wooded tunnel. Pass the entrance to **Manor Beacon**, cross the next road and follow the path between bracken and hedges. Make for a waymarked junction of paths and go straight on, keeping several gates on the right.

> **WHERE TO EAT AND DRINK** ⓘ
> The **Queen's Oak** is handy for a drink and something to eat. Snacks and other fare are available and there is a large enclosed beer garden at the side, pleasantly shaded by trees.

Follow the clear path as it cuts between fields and through woodland. Keep alongside a hedgerow to a stile and out to a lane. Cross over to a kissing gate and skirt the field, keeping the fence on your immediate right. Head for a gate ahead, pass between trees to the road and turn right. Bear left at the sign for **Vann House** and follow the track to **Fleethill Farm**. Keep to the left of the outbuildings, head for a stile and continue alongside the woodland edge to a stile in the field corner. Bear left after a few paces and follow the path between trees, joining a drive on the edge of Finchampstead.

This stretch of the walk is along an ancient road. According to some sources, it was here, in November 1501, that Henry VII and his sons Arthur and Henry, rode to meet Catherine of Aragon following her arrival from Spain. The King and the two princes had been hunting near by when they learnt that Catherine had reached Henry's hunting lodge at Dogmersfield.

Years earlier, Henry VII had dreamed of a marriage alliance with Spain. The youngest daughter of Ferdinand and Isabella of Spain,

Catherine was born in December 1485. She was just nine months older than Prince Arthur. When Catherine was nearly three years old, a treaty was signed which permitted them to marry when they were both of a suitable age. A member of the enormously powerful Spanish royal family, Catherine was addressed as 'the Princess of Wales' from a very early age. She spent many years preparing for the day when she would finally leave Spain and set sail for England.

> ### WHILE YOU'RE THERE
> Step into **Finchampstead church**, built on an ancient earthwork with a steep scarp on three sides. The brick tower was either replaced or rebuilt and over the chancel arch are fragments of 12th- and 15th-century wall paintings.

Eventually that day dawned, and in September 1501, Catherine began her journey. She would never return to her native Spain. On her arrival at Plymouth, she heard Mass and gave thanks for her safe passage. Meanwhile, a messenger began the lengthy journey to the King's residence at Easthampstead to inform his majesty that the long wait was over.

When word eventually reached Henry and his two sons, they made their way to Dogmersfield, arriving there on the evening of 4 November. But Catherine had

> ### WHAT TO LOOK FOR
> Close to the Queen's Oak is another royal connection. Encased by creeper is a **plaque** which reads: 'The oak tree near this stone was planted 21 June 1887 in commemoration of Queen Victoria's completion of the 50th year of her reign'. The stone was placed here in June 1897 to mark her Diamond Jubilee.

retired for the night and would see no one. Deeply suspicious, Henry insisted on seeing her and eventually his wish was granted. Lifting her veil, he was relieved to discover Catherine was a pretty girl, with red gold hair, blue eyes and a fair complexion. Henry thought she was a perfect bride for Arthur.

Ten days later, on 14 November, 1501, Catherine and Arthur were married in St Paul's Cathedral. He was just 15 and she was nearly 16. Little did Catherine realise what lay ahead. Arthur died six months after the wedding and his father passed Catherine on to his younger son, Henry, who duly married his brother's widow in 1509. As the Church forbade such a union, a special dispensation was obtained from the Pope. By about 1527, Henry, now King, was desperate for an heir, but all his children by Catherine, with the exception of one, had died in infancy. Having met and fallen in love with Anne Boleyn, Henry VIII was anxious to dissolve his marriage as soon as possible. The Pope refused to bow to his wishes and it was this decision that eventually triggered the Reformation in England.

Take the first left turning, passing alongside a fence and beneath the boughs of holly trees. Turn left by the garage and walk along to a drive on the right for **Rectory Farm**. Follow it to a stile and path to the right of the main gate, bear right after about 60yds (55m) and cut between paddocks. Cross the next stile, followed by a footbridge, turn left, then right. Swing left at the next junction and head for **Finchampstead church**. Cut through the churchyard and return to the **Queen's Oak**.

A Walk on the Wilde Side of Reading

Enjoy a heritage trail that explores the heart of Berkshire's county town, following stretches of the Thames and the Kennet and Avon Canal.

•DISTANCE•	3 miles (4.8km)
•MINIMUM TIME•	1hr 15min
•ASCENT / GRADIENT•	Negligible
•LEVEL OF DIFFICULTY•	
•PATHS•	Pavements, river and canal tow path, no stiles
•LANDSCAPE•	Urban
•SUGGESTED MAP•	aqua3 OS Explorer 159 Reading, Wokingham & Pangbourne. A good street map of Reading
•START / FINISH•	Grid reference: SU 716735
•DOG FRIENDLINESS•	On lead in town, under control on riverbank
•PARKING•	Reading Station, Chatham Street, Garrard Street, Hexagon
•PUBLIC TOILETS•	Reading Station

BACKGROUND TO THE WALK

Reading's skyline has changed dramatically over the years – riverside office developments have taken the place of many of the older buildings and the vast, new Oracle shopping complex is now the glittering jewel in the town centre's crown. However, some of old Reading's landmarks remain – and one of them is the town's gaol where Oscar Wilde languished for 18 months, between November 1895 and May 1897.

Importance of Being Oscar

It was the 8th Marquess of Queensberry, frustrated by his thwarted attempts to break up the scandalous relationship between his son, Lord Alfred Douglas, and Wilde, who was responsible for the writer's downward spiral into prison. He had publicly insulted Wilde, at his home, at his clubs and throughout London's theatreland where many of Wilde's plays were being performed.

Caught in the crossfire between father and son, Wilde brought a prosecution for libel against Queensberry, though he lost the case. Queensberry and his cohorts now began plotting to destroy Wilde once and for all. They gave evidence against him, testifying to his dubious sexuality and improper practices. The 1885 Criminal Law Amendment Act made sexual relations even between consenting males illegal and, not surprisingly, Wilde was found guilty as charged.

After two short spells in London prisons, Wilde was transferred to Reading Gaol. By now his physical condition had deteriorated and he was depressed and confused. A 'softer' prison with a less harsh regime was the obvious answer. Impressed by Wilde's reputation as a gifted writer, the governor made arrangements for him to work in the garden and the prison library. But life was still very tough in gaol.

If prison's dreary routine was hard for Wilde, things were not much better for him on the outside. His books were withdrawn from sale, his name was removed from theatre posters and he was declared bankrupt. Wilde had been ostracised. On his release, he was philosophical about his time in prison. It had given him time to study himself and there had certainly been long periods of soul-searching – 'that might bring balm to the bruised heart, and peace to the soul in pain', he wrote to Lord Alfred Douglas.

Each Man Kills the Thing He Loves

While in prison, Wilde wrote *The Ballad of Reading Gaol* (published in 1898), about a man hanged there for the murder of his wife. The execution cast a long shadow over the inmates, and Wilde in particular, but this work, more than any other, gave him status as a writer of serious merit.

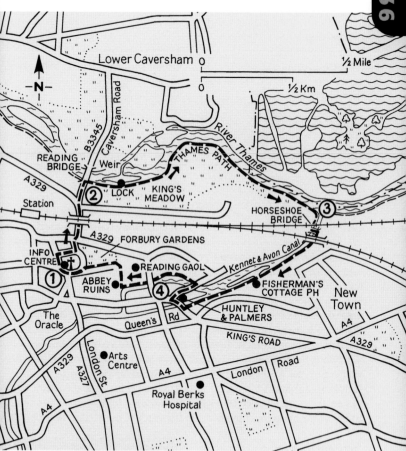

Walk 36 Directions

① Start by the statue of Queen Victoria and, with your back to the **Town Hall**, turn right, pass the tourist information centre and the museum. Cross **Valpy Street** and

turn right into **Forbury Road**. Walk down to the roundabout, where the **Rising Sun** pub is seen on the corner, and turn left towards the railway bridge. Pass beneath the line and cross the road at the pedestrian lights. Avoid King's Meadow Road and make for **Reading Bridge**.

Walk 36

② Take the steps on the right just before the bridge and join the **Thames Path**, heading downstream with the river on your left. Pass **Caversham Lock** as the sound of traffic begins to fade and the surroundings becomes leafier. Skirt **King's Meadow,** with smart apartment buildings and lines of houses on the opposite bank. Pass a boat yard, full of cabin cruisers and narrow boats, and continue under the branches of trees. Eventually reach **Kennet Mouth** and here a distinctive Sustrans waymark directs you over the bridge (in the direction of Bristol!).

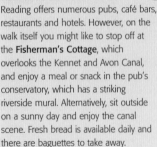

> **WHERE TO EAT AND DRINK** ⓘ
> Reading offers numerous pubs, café bars, restaurants and hotels. However, on the walk itself you might like to stop off at the **Fisherman's Cottage**, which overlooks the Kennet and Avon Canal, and enjoy a meal or snack in the pub's conservatory, which has a striking riverside mural. Alternatively, sit outside on a sunny day and enjoy the canal scene. Fresh bread is available daily and there are baguettes to take away.

Reading Gas Company in 1880. Join the tow path and keep the vast hulk of the Prudential building over on the left bank.

> **WHILE YOU'RE THERE** ⓘ
> Visit the **Museum of Reading**, next door to the tourist information centre. Here you can see a full size replica of the Bayeux Tapestry, discover artefacts from the Roman town of Silchester and learn about the history of Huntley and Palmers, Reading's famous biscuit factory.

③ Cross **Horseshoe Bridge** and turn left on the far side, heading for central Reading. Pass beneath Brunel's railway bridge, continue to the **Fisherman's Cottage** and **Blakes Lock**, and leave the canal tow path at the next bridge. Turn right along **King's Road**, passing the wonderful listed façade of the Huntley and Palmer's biscuit factory, then turn immediately right and cross the bridge built by the

④ Pass under **King's Road**, keep to the right and follow **Chestnut Walk**. **Reading Gaol**, where Oscar Wilde was imprisoned, can be seen over to the right. Walk along to the ruins of **Reading Abbey** and turn right. Keep alongside the gaol and enter **Forbury Gardens** through a flint arch. Keep to the left edge, with the statue of the lion, erected to commemorate the 19th-century imperial campaigns in Afghanistan, on your right. Look for the abbey gateway on the left, with **Reading Crown Court** adjacent, and exit at Victoria Gate. Walk ahead to the outer gate of Reading Abbey, pass the **Church of St Laurence-in-Reading** on the right and return to the tourist information centre and the statue at the start of the walk.

> **WHAT TO LOOK FOR** ⓘ
> **Horseshoe Bridge** is where the Kennet and the Thames meet. Earley Wharf once stood on this site – and it may have been used by the Romans to serve their local town of Silchester, on the Berkshire/Hampshire border. Threatened by several road schemes over the years, Kennet Mouth and the bridge were saved by a campaign fought by those who value this historic corner of Reading. **Reading Abbey** was established by Henry I and its history is recorded on the wall outside. Henry VIII sealed its fate with the Dissolution of the monasteries. The last abbot, Hugh Faringdon, protested in the most vigorous terms, was charged with high treason, found guilty and hanged. The buildings were desecrated during the Civil War and today little remains of the original abbey.

A Fashionable Riverside Resort at Pangbourne

Journey to the peaceful waters of the Pang before heading for the Thames Path and a National Trust meadow.

•DISTANCE•	3 miles (4.8km)
•MINIMUM TIME•	1hr 30min
•ASCENT / GRADIENT•	Negligible
•LEVEL OF DIFFICULTY•	
•PATHS•	Field and riverside paths, stretches of road, section of Thames Path, 4 stiles
•LANDSCAPE•	Gentle farmland on banks of Pang and Thames
•SUGGESTED MAP•	aqua3 OS Explorer 159 Reading, Wokingham & Pangbourne
•START / FINISH•	Grid reference: SU 633765
•DOG FRIENDLINESS•	On lead in Pangbourne, under control on farmland and by River Thames
•PARKING•	Car park off A329 in Pangbourne, near railway bridge
•PUBLIC TOILETS•	At car park

BACKGROUND TO THE WALK

During the Edwardian era the Thames-side settlement of Pangbourne became especially fashionable with artists, writers and anglers, yet apparently it did little to ignite the interest of one renowned literary figure. 'Pleasant house, hate Pangbourne, nothing happens', wrote D H Lawrence (▶ Walk 42) in 1919 when he and his wife rented a cottage in the village.

Popular Pangbourne

On the other hand, D H Evans, who founded the famous West End department store, clearly found Pangbourne to his liking. Towards the end of the 19th century he built seven very distinctive villas in the village. Known as the Seven Deadly Sins and distinguished by domes, turrets, balconies and gables, the villas were not popular with everyone.

There were those who claimed the seven villas had been built to house Evans' seven mistresses, while others believed he lived in a different one each day of the week. Lady Cunard, noted for her notorious parties, bought one of the houses. One local resident claimed the parties were riotous and wild, adding 'anything would have seemed wild compared to life in Pangbourne'.

Without the river, Pangbourne would hardly have gained its reputation as an inland resort. The spacious meadows, glorious hanging woods and varied assortment of pubs and hotels have made the village one of the most popular destinations on this stretch of the Thames. One man whose love for this river lasted a lifetime was Kenneth Grahame. He wrote *The Wind in the Willows* in 1908 and found the inspiration for this delightful story here. Grahame was born in 1859 and first came to live in Berkshire when he was five. His strength lay in his ability to create a magical world for children, providing a fascinating insight into a child's imagination and their view of the puzzling adult world.

Walk 37

Grahame and his wife became parents rather late in life and it was their son's bedtime stories, as well as letters sent to the boy by his father while away on holiday, that formed the basis for Grahame's classic *The Wind in the Willows*. Both father and son drew on their love of the Berkshire countryside and its wild creatures to complete the story. Having lived for much of his life in the Thames Valley, Grahame eventually moved to Pangbourne in 1924, buying Church Cottage in the centre of the village. His beloved Thames was only a short walk away and he died here in 1932.

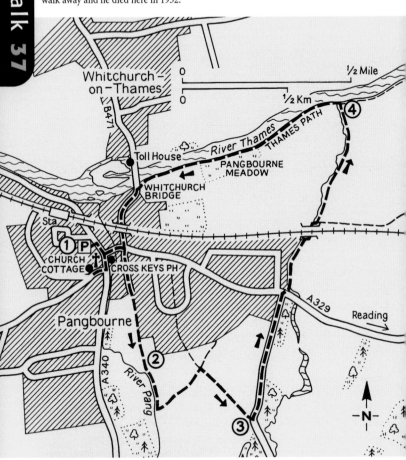

Walk 37 Directions

① From the car park turn right to the mini-roundabout and walk along to the church and adjoining **Church Cottage**. Retrace your steps to the main road, keep the **Cross Keys** pub on the right and turn right at the mini-roundabout. Cross the **Pang** and bear right at the next

major junction into **The Moors**. At the end of the drive continue ahead on a waymarked footpath. Pass alongside various houses and gardens and patches of scrub, then go through a pretty tunnel of trees. Further on is a gate with a local map and an information board about the area. Beyond the gate the River Pang can be seen sweeping in from the right.

Walk 37

WHAT TO LOOK FOR

Church Cottage, Kenneth Grahame's home, is next door to St James the Less. The house looks much the same today as it did in Grahame's day, with the little round village lock-up, which he used as a tool shed, in the garden. Towards the end of the walk, as you leave the riverbank, look out for **Whitchurch Bridge**, a Victorian iron toll bridge distinguished by its white lattice architecture. Cars pay to cross the bridge but pedestrians go free. Before decimalization, they were charged ½d. The bridge is privately owned.

② Follow the riverside path, with white willow trees seen on the bank. Make for a footbridge. Don't cross it, instead, turn sharp left and walk across the open meadow to a stile in the far boundary. Once over it, keep alongside the hedge on the left and, as you approach a Second World War pill box, turn right at a path intersection and cross a footbridge. Head for another footbridge on the far side of the field and then look for a third bridge with white railings, by the field boundary. Cross the bridge and the stile beyond it and then head across the field to the far boundary.

③ Exit to the road and bear left. Follow the lane between hedges and oak trees and walk along to the **A329**. Go diagonally right to the footpath by the sign for Purley Rise and follow the path north towards distant trees. Turn right at the next bridge and follow the concrete track as it bends left to run beneath the railway line. Once through it, bear right to a stile and then follow the track along the left edge of the field, beside a rivulet. Ahead on the horizon are glorious hanging woods on the north bank of the **Thames**. Pass double galvanised gates and a bridge on the left and continue on the footpath as it crosses this gentle lowland landscape. Cross a stile and walk across the next field to reach the riverbank.

WHERE TO EAT AND DRINK

Pangbourne boasts several inns, hotels and restaurants. The **Cross Keys**, opposite the church, is one of the oldest pubs and has plenty of character. There are several bars and quaint low ceilings, as well as a patio running down to the River Pang, a popular feature in summer.

④ On reaching the **River Thames**, turn left and head towards **Pangbourne**. Follow the **Thames Path** to **Pangbourne Meadow** and up ahead now is **Whitchurch Bridge**. As you approach it, begin to veer away from the riverbank towards a car park. Keep left when you get to the road, pass beneath the railway line and turn right at the next junction. Bear right again at the mini-roundabout and return to the car park.

WHILE YOU'RE THERE

Enjoy a leisurely stroll across **Pangbourne Meadow** or even pause here to watch the colourful boating activity on the river. In the summer, the Thames is alive with gin palaces and cabin cruisers. The meadow, covering an area of about 7 acres (3ha), is in the care of the National Trust. Pangbourne's **Church of St James the Less** is distinguished by its square tower and battlements which tend to dominate the skyline. It is the second, if not the third church to occupy this site. Kenneth Grahame's funeral took place here in July 1932 and was recorded in *The Times*. Children from all over the country sent flowers and there were willows gathered from the river that morning. His body was later moved to Holywell Cemetery in Oxford, where he lies beside his son.

Frilsham and a Classic Country Pub

On a warm summer's day, this delightful woodland walk offers plenty of welcome shade.

•DISTANCE•	3½ miles (5.7km)
•MINIMUM TIME•	1hr 30min
•ASCENT / GRADIENT•	99ft (30m) ▲▲▲
•LEVEL OF DIFFICULTY•	🚶 🚶 🚶
•PATHS•	Tracks, paths and stretches of country road, no stiles
•LANDSCAPE•	Woodland on northern side of Pang Valley
•SUGGESTED MAP•	aqua3 OS Explorer 158 Newbury & Hungerford
•START / FINISH•	Grid reference: SU 551731
•DOG FRIENDLINESS•	Under control on Yattendon Estate
•PARKING•	Space at side of Pot Kiln
•PUBLIC TOILETS•	None on route

BACKGROUND TO THE WALK

Sadly, in some English pubs the familiar call 'time Gentlemen please' has assumed a new significance in recent years. It isn't just the deregulation of licensing laws which threatens to make this age-old publican's cry redundant, but the very continued existance of the traditional public house. One of England's greatest institutions has been under threat for some time, and yet it remains an integral part of rural and urban life. It would be hard to imagine a world without it.

The Birth of the English Pub

Our pubs are unique to this country but how exactly did they begin? The story of the English pub spans more than 1,000 years of history, beginning with the dismal alehouses of the Anglo-Saxon period. Later came the old drovers' hostelries, followed by coaching inns and then Georgian and Victorian pubs built to take advantage of the canal and railway trade. Finally, today, we have the familiar theme boozer and the up-market restaurant establishment, neither of which bear much resemblance to the traditional image of the genuine, authentic local.

Preserving Tradition

It's hard to find a pub that hasn't been altered in one way or another. Many have gone altogether, sold off for development or converted into private houses, while others have made subtle changes to meet the demands of the modern world. And those that appear not to have changed in any way have almost certainly been very clever and tapped into a niche market. Preserving a pub by retaining its antique tills and fading wallpaper, giving the impression it belongs in some sort of fossilized time warp like a museum piece, often produces dividends. The landlord may deliberately chose not to move with the times, knowing that the look, feel and atmosphere of his pub conveys the right impression and that it is what many people want.

Traditional Local

One such pub belonging in this particular category is the Pot Kiln, a famous tavern in an isolated part of Berkshire. Until the beginning of the Second World War, there were brick kilns in this area – hence the name of the pub. Hidden among trees, the Pot Kiln is superbly located down a narrow country lane and is quite hard to find. In fact, there is not another house in sight. There have been many additions and various changes to the inn over the years, but, thankfully, the Pot Kiln still retains its original character. Many of its supporters feel it should have a protection order slapped on it, so that it can be preserved for all time as a permanent reminder of how country pubs used to be.

From the outside, the inn could almost pass for a farm or a private house. Inside, there are two bars – lounge and public – and between them is an off-sales hatch in the panelled lobby. The lounge bar has tables and bar stools, bench seats and a log fire in winter. In 2001 the landlords celebrated 20 years at the Pot Kiln – an excellent testimony to their success.

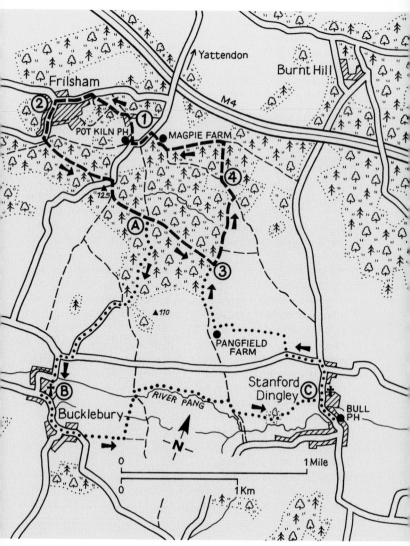

Walk 38 Directions

① Go to the end of the car park at the side of the **Pot Kiln** and follow the track. Keep the microbrewery on your left and pass several houses, including **Laurel Bank Cottages**. Avoid a public footpath on the left and continue to two cottages at right angles to the byway. Bear left just beyond them and follow a footpath between holly trees. Disregard the turning on the left and keep right at the next fork. Head for the road and turn left. Walk through **Frilsham** village, pass **Beechfield**, a residential development, and turn left at the sign for Hermitage and Bucklebury.

> **WHILE YOU'RE THERE** ⓘ
> At the rear of the Pot Kiln is the **West Berkshire Brewery**, a microbrewery set up in 1995 to cater for many country pubs in the area. The beers at the Pot Kiln are brewed here and groups of at least a dozen visitors can tour the site by appointment. The West Berkshire Brewery supplied four firkins (36 gallons/164 litres) of ale to British troops in Turkey and Oman in 2001.

② When the lane bends right, go straight ahead, following the path deep into the woods. Pass through a gate and continue on the bridleway to the next waymark. Branch off to the left at this point, following the path down the wooded slope to the road. Cross over to a gateway and continue ahead on the track. Piles of logs can often be seen lining the route, waiting to be transported to the sawmills. Pass a waymarked track on the right and continue on the main track, following it through ornamental woodland to the next waymarked junction.

③ Bear left here and cut through bluebell woods to a gate. Cross the field to a gate in the next boundary, with traffic on the M4 visible in the distance. Veer half left in the field and away to the right in the distance, you can just make out the façade of Yattendon Court, up among the trees. Cross the field and make for a bridleway on the right, running into the trees.

> **WHERE TO EAT AND DRINK** ⓘ
> The **Pot Kiln** (► Background to the Walk) is ideal for liquid refreshment or a pub lunch at the end of the walk. A summer evening is also a good time to relax over a pint in the garden before sampling the menu inside. Filled rolls are a perennial favourite.

④ Beyond the wood, follow the path between fences and swing left at the next waymarked junction. Walk along to the next junction, where there are footpath and bridleway signs, and veer right. Follow the track round the side of **Magpie Farm** and on reaching the road, turn left. Return to the car park by the **Pot Kiln**.

> **WHAT TO LOOK FOR** ⓘ
> The Yattendon Estate supplies **Christmas trees** to places from Land's End to John o'Groats, and with more than 1.8 million trees planted over 600 acres (243ha), it is one of Britain's biggest producers. Around 150,000 Christmas trees are sold here every year. Walking through the estate reveals the sheer scale and size of the operation.

The Bull at Stanford Dingley

Follow pretty woodland paths down into the Pang Valley.
See map and information panel for Walk 38

•DISTANCE•	8 miles (12.9km)
•MINIMUM TIME•	3hrs 45min
•ASCENT / GRADIENT•	95ft (29m) ▲▲▲
•LEVEL OF DIFFICULTY•	🚶 🚶 🚶

Walk 39 Directions
(Walk 38 option)

After crossing the lane between Points ② and ③ in Walk 38, follow the track and turn right at the waymarked junction, Point Ⓐ. Go straight on at the next waymark and eventually reach a drive by a house. Walk down to the road and bear right. Turn left at the next junction, towards **Bucklebury**. Cross the **Pang** and go straight ahead, through a gate and across the field to the church, Point Ⓑ.

On leaving the church, keep left and head towards a timber-framed cottage. Exit to the road and turn left. Take the next left-hand right of way, opposite the **School House**. Follow a grassy track and three-quarters of the way across a field, reach the corner of a ditch and a waymark. Turn left here and head for a stile. Continue ahead in the next field and make for a bridge, turning right to follow the Pang to **Stanford Dingley**.

Cross a stile and then keep ahead on a waterside path, eventually reaching two stiles, a gate and a track. Bear right here for about 80yds (73m) to the next gateway,

swinging left immediately before it. Keep left as the path forks, making for a stile among the trees in the far corner. Cross a wood to the next stile and then follow the path across the pasture, keeping **Stanford Dingley church** in view. Make for a stile at the road and turn right to visit the **Bull**, Point Ⓒ, another classic pub.

This village inn dates back to the 15th century and includes a wealth of original timbers as well as the remains of an original wattle and daub wall. One of its more unusual features is the traditional, and now quite rare, pub game known as ring-the-bull, involving a genuine surviving bull's ring.

To continue the walk, keep left and head away from the village. Take the first left turning, signposted 'Bucklebury'. As the road begins to curve left, look for a path and stile on the right and enter the field. Follow the boundary to a stile and walk ahead across the next field, aiming to the right of **Pangfield Farm**. As you draw level with the outbuildings, take the permissive path on the right. Join the right of way further along and follow it through the woodland. Keep ahead to the next waymarked junction and rejoin Walk 38 at Point ③.

Walk 40

In Praise of Douai

Enjoy a quiet country walk and visit a magnificent newly-built abbey church.

•**DISTANCE**•	3 miles (4.8km)
•**MINIMUM TIME**•	1hr 30min
•**ASCENT / GRADIENT**•	90ft (27m) ▲ ▲ ▲
•**LEVEL OF DIFFICULTY**•	🚶🚶 🚶🚶 🚶🚶
•**PATHS**•	Tracks, field and woodland paths, stretches of village road and country lane
•**LANDSCAPE**•	Mixture of woodland and farmland on south-facing slopes of Kennet Valley
•**SUGGESTED MAP**•	aqua3 OS Explorer 159 Reading, Wokingham & Pangbourne
•**START / FINISH**•	Grid reference: SU 586688
•**DOG FRIENDLINESS**•	On lead in Beenham, near Douai and near livestock, under control on woodland stretches
•**PARKING**•	Small car park by Victory Hall
•**PUBLIC TOILETS**•	None on route

Walk 40 **Directions**

From the car park turn right and follow the road through **Beenham** to **Clay Lane**. Veer left and left again by **Jayswood Cottage**. Follow the byway and pass the entrance to **Oakwood Farm**. When the track curves left, swing right at the bridleway sign. Cross a stream and turn left. Follow the path round the field, climbing by woods to the road, emerging by the entrance to **Malthouse Farm**.

Head up the road towards **Douai Abbey** and look for a footpath on the left, leading across the playing field to **St Peter's Church** at **Woolhampton**. Keep to the left of the pavilion and look for the gate into the churchyard. Turn right at the road, pass the school and follow the road round the right bend. At the main entrance to Douai Abbey, bear left by some thatched cottages and pass the abbey church.

Work on this splendid building began in 1928 and the east end was completed in 1933. However, it was the summer of 1993 before the church was completed, opened and dedicated. The original design, by Arnold Crush, can be seen in the choir and sanctuary areas. The initial plan was to have a transept crossing surmounted by a tower, and, with another seven bays, the church would have extended almost to the road.

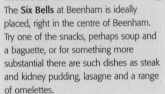

WHERE TO EAT AND DRINK ⓘ
The **Six Bells** at Beenham is ideally placed, right in the centre of Beenham. Try one of the snacks, perhaps soup and a baguette, or for something more substantial there are such dishes as steak and kidney pudding, lasagne and a range of omelettes.

When, years after work began, circumstances eventually allowed its completion, the monastic community at Douai chose to finish the church in a style that suited the

WHAT TO LOOK FOR ⓘ

Next to Woolhampton church lie the buildings of **Elstree School**, a famous preparatory school that moved to this site from Elstree in Hertfordshire in 1939, to avoid the threat of bombing. Prior to that, the house had been the country seat of Count Dudley Melchior Beaumont Gurowski, son of an Austrian consul.

modern age, with the focus on prayer and praise. In 1987 Dr Michael Blee was invited to start work on a new design.

Step inside and you'll spot several notable memorials. One is to pupils of the former school killed in the world wars, while another commemorates all those who contributed to the building of the new church. The chapel to the north was originally dedicated to St Benedict and is now the Blessed Sacrament Chapel, used for private prayer and worship. The altar here is the work of Thomas Derrick, with the inscription by Eric Gill.

The church may be new but what of Douai's history? The abbey community covers more than three and a half centuries. The Dissolution of the monasteries during the reign of Henry VIII drove men and women who opted for a monastic existence to flee abroad. In 1615 a group of English monks gathered in Paris to form the community of St Edmund. Other English monasteries were formed there and together they restored the English Benedictine Congregation, first established in 1336.

Having been suppressed and almost extinguished by the events of the French Revolution, the survivors of St Edmund's moved, in 1818, to Douai in France. However, their

future was far from certain. In 1903 the monks were again expelled from their monastery on anti-clerical grounds. This time they crossed the channel to Berkshire, taking the name 'Douai' with them. They took over the existing St Mary's College, transforming it into a leading Roman Catholic public school for boys, which closed in 1999.

These days the Douai community includes around 30 monks, who receive guests here, host conferences and offer a place of retreat. They also help organise events in the church itself and in other parts of the abbey campus, as well as working in the surrounding parish.

Beyond the church, continue along the road to some cottages and barns. Turn right at a footpath sign and follow the track into the next field. Keep to the field edge and when you reach the corner, by the footpath sign, go straight over into the woods. Fields can be seen close by on the left. Follow the path through the trees and eventually reach the outskirts of **Beenham**.

Turn left at the junction, then right by **Jayswood Cottage**, back into the centre of the village. The **Six Bells** pub is on the left and the car park, where the walk began, is near by.

WHILE YOU'RE THERE ⓘ

St Peter's Church at Woolhampton was completely Gothicised in the mid-19th century. The roof and main walls of the old church were retained and the walls encased in flint. The old bell tower was also transformed into an attractive shingled spire. John Betjeman is reputed to have visited the church and was so impressed by its attractive rural setting that he urged the villagers to fight off any proposal to develop the area.

Enduring Brimpton

A walk through Wasing Park to Brimpton overlooking the Kennet Valley.

•DISTANCE•	6 miles (9.7km)
•MINIMUM TIME•	2hrs 45min
•ASCENT / GRADIENT•	150ft (46m) ▲▲ ▲ ▲
•LEVEL OF DIFFICULTY•	林林 林林 林林
•PATHS•	Field and woodland paths and tracks, parkland drives, meadow, road and riverside, 11 stiles
•LANDSCAPE•	Common, parkland, woodland and meadow
•SUGGESTED MAP•	aqua3 OS Explorer 159 Reading, Wokingham & Pangbourne
•START / FINISH•	Grid reference: SU 567628
•DOG FRIENDLINESS•	On lead in Wasing Park and Ashford Hill Meadows
•PARKING•	Limited spaces in lay-by opposite Pineapple pub
•PUBLIC TOILETS•	None on route

BACKGROUND TO THE WALK

The English village is one of the key elements that have helped to shape the rural character of this country over the centuries. England's village communities are etched into the fabric of its society, reflecting a way of life that is the envy of others.

Typical Village

However, there has been concern in recent years that some of the time-honoured traditions are being eroded. As we begin the 21st century, so we move into an era of even greater social upheaval. But the village is such a vital and integral part of our rural landscape that, despite the tide of change, it is likely to survive through the next century and beyond – though, almost certainly, in a different form.

Berkshire, like Buckinghamshire, is blessed with many fine villages that, thankfully, have stood the test of time and remained largely intact. Some have fallen victim to planning blight and seen their boundaries expanded in recent years, while others have successfully fought off late 20th-century development, their pride and spirit intact.

One such village that has so far avoided change is Brimpton, just to the south of the A4, between Newbury and Reading. Bounded to the north by the River Kennet and to the south by the lesser-known Enborne, Brimpton, in the main, lies at the end of a breezy ridge. As a village, it's like hundreds of others around the country. But it is that similarity that makes it a typical English rural community. Look closely and you'll see that its key component parts remain in place – the shop and post office, the public house, the primary school and the church are all here.

Village records reveal a fascinating insight into how Brimpton has changed and evolved over the years into the community you see today. As with most rural settlements, Brimpton was once part of the feudal system, shaped and controlled by landowning families, aristocrats and local benefactors. In 1854 the Countess of Falmouth built almshouses for elderly couples and widows, while the Earl donated a small piece of land on which to build a school. Later, when the church was rebuilt, the local squire, James Blyth, objected to the pub being near the church and gave land for a new site.

The local shop was once the home of Duncan McClean, who moved here in 1920. Blinded in the First World War, McClean was a basket and net maker, as well as a poultry farmer. In later years his wife established the village stores. Nearby Glebe Cottage was once known as The Brimpton Refreshment Rooms. Brimpton's villagers, today, are proud of their community. So much so that an illustrated map of the village and its history was unveiled outside the church – marking the new millennium.

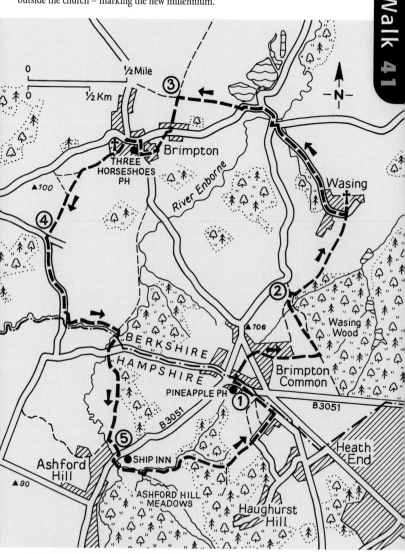

Walk 41 **Directions**

① Follow the path across two stiles to the road. Cross over to join a byway, follow it round to the right

and across the **common**. When it swings sharp left, go straight on along the path. Take the path to the right of **Woodside**, bear left at a T-junction and follow the path. Where it joins a track, veer off left at a waymark, following the field-edge path. Look for an opening in the trees ahead, cross a bridge and turn right at a track, following it to a sign for **Wasing Church**.

② Take the track, turn left at the bend and cut through the wood. Cross a drive to visit the church, return to the drive, turn right and follow it down to the road. Bear left to a junction, then right over the **Enborne** to a fork. Keep left and turn right at the Wasing Estate sign. Veer left along a grassy track to a junction and bear left.

> ### WHILE YOU'RE THERE ℹ
> Step briefly off the path to look at **Wasing church**, adjacent to the main house. Distinguished by its weatherboarded bell turret and pyramid roof, the church is mainly 15th century and was rebuilt in 1761. Wasing Park is the family seat of the Mount family – look for the dates of Sir William Mount and his wife on the churchyard gates.

③ Follow the path to the road, turn right for several paces, then left to join the next path. Keep over to the left edge of the field, go through a kissing gate in the top corner and veer right. Turn right to reach a housing estate. Bear right at the road and walk along to the church, following the path beside it. On reaching a field corner, go straight on, swinging left by power lines. Head south to **Hyde End Lane**.

④ Turn left, keeping right at the fork. Look for a stile to the left of a footbridge and cross a meadow. Follow the riverbank to a footbridge and stile. Cross over and take the path to a stile and bridge. Cross the road and follow the track, taking the path to the left of it along the woodland edge and making for a bridge in the far right corner of the field. Follow a line of trees to a stile and cross the next pasture towards buildings. Approaching a gate and a cottage, veer left to a stile. Cross to another stile by the road.

> ### WHAT TO LOOK FOR ℹ
> **Ashford Hill Meadows** is a delightful area to explore on foot. The English Nature site is managed by traditional hay cutting and grazing and includes damp meadows, dry grasslands and areas of shrub and woodland. A range of habitats supports an outstanding variety of flowers and insects.

⑤ Turn right over the bridge and bear left to a gate leading into **Ashford Hill Meadows**, veering left across pastures. After 75 yds (68m) it becomes enclosed by trees, look closely for a fork and branch off left to a footbridge. Begin crossing a field and after about 120yds (109m), make for a gate on the left. Swing right and keep left at the fork after about 50yds (45m). Look for a stile at the fence corner and follow the path up through the trees. Head for a stile, turn left and cross the field to the next stile. Go straight ahead along a lane and when it bends right, bear left and follow the path to the road. Continue ahead, returning to the lay-by by the inn.

> ### WHERE TO EAT AND DRINK ℹ
> The **Pineapple**, at the start and finish of the walk, is a picturesque thatched pub. There is some uncertainty over its name. Where the pineapple comes from, no one really knows! Inside are low ceilings, quarry tiled floors, beams and fireplaces, giving it a cosy, intimate feel. The **Three Horseshoes** at Brimpton is a village local. with a choice of snacks and main meals. Alternatively, you might like to wait until you get to the **Ship Inn**, which also has a post office at the rear of the building.

Hermitage – a Writer's Wartime Refuge

Explore dense woodland and pass the former home of a famous British novelist on this spectacular walk near Newbury.

•DISTANCE•	6 miles (9.7km)
•MINIMUM TIME•	2hrs 45min
•ASCENT / GRADIENT•	320ft (98m) ▲▲ ▲ ▲
•LEVEL OF DIFFICULTY•	👫 👫 👫
•PATHS•	Field and woodland paths and tracks, some road, 4 stiles
•LANDSCAPE•	Extensive woodland with areas of open farmland
•SUGGESTED MAP•	aqua3 OS Explorer 158 Newbury & Hungerford
•START / FINISH•	Grid reference: SU 505730
•DOG FRIENDLINESS•	Under control in woods and on lead near livestock
•PARKING•	Limited parking in Hermitage
•PUBLIC TOILETS•	None on route

BACKGROUND TO THE WALK

It is a little-known fact that one of Britain's most famous and outspoken 20th-century writers lived quietly in a Berkshire village at the end of the First World War. What is even more surprising is that he and his wife deliberately chose a low profile. But why? What drove them to seek refuge in the depths of the English countryside?

D H Lawrence

During the early years of the First World War David Herbert Lawrence (1885–1930) and his German bride Frieda lived near St Ives in Cornwall, but were not accepted by the local community. In remote rural areas, women such as Lawrence's wife were often looked upon with suspicion and hatred. The war had been long and bloody and Frieda, living among people who had lost friends and loved ones, was an unwelcome reminder of Germany's part in it. In one among several letters signalling his concern, Lawrence wrote: 'Sudden blow! We are served with notice to leave the area of Cornwall by Monday next... by the military. It is a complete mystery to me – complete.'

Move to Berkshire

Forced to leave Cornwall, the couple moved to Hermitage near Newbury in December 1917, renting a small cottage from a friend. It was a quiet and peaceful place but even here Lawrence and his wife were not left alone. While living at Chapel Farm Cottage, they received regular calls from the police. To make matters worse, Lawrence was a pacifist and openly opposed the war. Ill health gave him a genuine reason not to fight, but his outspoken views and choice of bride were hardly going to endear him to the villagers of Hermitage.

Walking All Day

However, Lawrence liked life in Berkshire. He would walk many miles in a day, often leaving home very early in the morning and not returning until late in the afternoon. He was able to combine his knowledge of the countryside with his skill as a writer, using prose and imagery to convey his love of creation. A keen artist and gardener, Lawrence would also write at great speed and it was while living at Chapel Farm Cottage that he undertook some revision of earlier work, including *Women in Love* (1921).

Prolific Writer

During the two years he lived at the cottage, Lawrence worked on various short stories, several novels and some poetry. Of all his writing, the story most closely associated with Hermitage is *The Fox*, first published in 1923 in *Three Novellas*. The story is set at Bailey Farm, which Lawrence based on Grimsbury Farm, just outside the village. The setting for the farm, the surrounding countryside and the nearby railway are all faithfully recreated in *The Fox*, while the nearby market town is undoubtedly Newbury. Lawrence left Hermitage for Italy in November 1919.

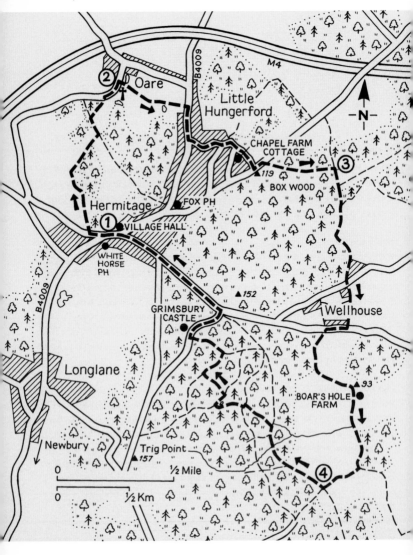

Walk 42 Directions

① From the village hall in Hermitage turn right, then right again into **Doctors Lane**. Cross a stile by a private road sign and head across the field to the next stile. Pass beneath power lines and make for a stile in the boundary of the woodland ahead of you. Follow the footpath through the trees as far as a cottage. Turn left when you reach the track and veer right after about 60yds (55m) at the public footpath sign. Drop down through the woodland to a lane and keep to the right. Walk along the lane to the hamlet of **Oare** and turn right by a small pond.

> **WHERE TO EAT AND DRINK** ⓘ
>
> Hermitage has two pubs – the **Fox** and the **White Horse**. Both are typical village locals offering a good range of beers and a selection of snacks and more substantial dishes.

② Head towards the buildings of **Little Hungerford**, cross a stile and turn right at the road. Bear left into **Chapel Lane** and follow the road round the right-hand bend. Pass **Pond Lane** and D H Lawrence's former home on the corner as you head for the next road junction. **Chapel Farm Cottage** is clearly identified – its front entrance is in Pond Lane and its rear garden backs on to Chapel Lane. Turn left and walk along to a public footpath sign on the right. Follow the track deep into **Box Wood** and eventually reach a junction.

③ Bear right here and follow the track through the trees to the next road. Cross over by a bungalow and continue on the next section of track. Turn right at the next road

and walk along to the turning for **Boar's Hole Farm** on the left. Follow the track to the farm and continue south to a left-hand bend. Go through the gate on the right and make for a gate and house in the field corner. Keep to the right of the house and turn right at a track bend, passing through a galvanised metal gate.

> **WHILE YOU'RE THERE** ⓘ
>
> Stop and look at **St Bartholomew's Church** at Oare, built on the site of a priory chapel. The priory was destroyed by Henry VIII, but its history is reflected in local place names such as Chapel Lane and Chapel Farm Cottage – where D H Lawrence and his wife lived. John Betjeman described the church as 'a Victorian gem set in the Berkshire countryside'. The history of Oare, from AD 968, is described inside.

④ Follow the woodland track and keep right at the fork. Cross a stream and pass a left turning. Take the next left path by a stream and pass over a staggered junction. Turn right by the pond, then first left, cutting through the trees. Swing right at the next junction and follow the track as it runs up by a seat. Keep left at the junction and make for the road by a cottage. Opposite are the earthworks of **Grimsbury Castle**. Turn right and walk along to the road junction. Bear left and return to Hermitage.

> **WHAT TO LOOK FOR** ⓘ
>
> **Grimsbury Castle** is a hill fort with its origins in the years preceding the Roman conquest. It's enclosed by a ramp, ditch and counterscarp bank. The north and west entrances have additional defences. Excavation work has revealed that it was occupied between the 3rd and 1st centuries BC. Across the road is an 18th-century battlemented tower.

Donnington Castle – a Vital Civil War Stronghold

Walk 43

Stroll through a country park to a castle overlooking the Kennet Valley.

•**DISTANCE**•	3 miles (4.8km)
•**MINIMUM TIME**•	1hr 45min
•**ASCENT / GRADIENT**•	165ft (50m) ▲▲ ▲ ▲
•**LEVEL OF DIFFICULTY**•	👫 👫 👫
•**PATHS**•	Paths and tracks through woods,
•**LANDSCAPE**•	Formal country park, golf course and woodland
•**SUGGESTED MAP**•	aqua3 OS Explorer 158 Newbury & Hungerford
•**START / FINISH**•	Grid reference: SU 463709
•**DOG FRIENDLINESS**•	Under control at Snelsmore Common and by golf course
•**PARKING**•	Car park at Snelsmore Common Country Park
•**PUBLIC TOILETS**•	Snelsmore Common Country Park

BACKGROUND TO THE WALK

On a hillside to the north of Newbury lie the remains of Donnington Castle, once a major stronghold commanding the key routes passing through the town – now the A4 and the A34. The castle's strategic importance was immense and was borne out by the prolonged fighting for it during the Civil War. Today, what remains of Donnington Castle looks down forlornly on a town that has spread its arms very widely since those days. But it is still an imposing monument.

A Long History

The manor of Deritone (now Donnington) was held by the Crown in 1086. In 1386 Richard II granted a licence to 'build anew' and crenellate Donnington Castle, to Sir Richard de Abberbury, a member of the royal household and former guardian of the King. Later, the castle passed to Thomas Chaucer, probably the son of the poet. By the time of Elizabeth I it was back in royal possession – there are accounts of the restoration work to the castle in preparation for her visit there in 1568. This included planking the bridge, mending chamber floors, building sheds for the kitchen and making tables, forms and trestles.

Civil War

At the time of the Civil War, Donnington Castle belonged to John Packer, whose refusal of a loan to the King and opposition in Parliament led to the sequestration of his property by Charles I. Colonel John Boys was sent to take command of the castle for the King in September 1643, with 200 foot soldiers, 25 horses and four pieces of cannon. He strengthened the defences of the castle by constructing the star fort earthworks around it, which can still be seen below the castle today. Boys withstood two Parliamentary assaults on the castle in July and September 1644 and was knighted by the King in October.

The Second Battle of Newbury, on 27 October 1644, was somewhat inconclusive, but the Royalist Army was able to slip away leaving the Crown, Great Seal and artillery in Boys' keeping at Donnington. Boys then withstood another siege by the Parliamentary army until relieved by the King on 9 November. Repeated attempts were made to take the castle, but Boys did not surrender until instructed to do so by the King on 1 April 1646. The outline of the castle can be seen today but the most impressive feature still standing is its magnificent gatehouse. The grounds of Donnington Castle are open every day of the week and on most weekends there are at least a handful of people surveying the ruins and gazing out across Newbury to the hills and downland beyond.

Walk 43

Walk 43 **Directions**

① Keep the toilet block on your right and walk ahead to a vehicle barrier and a sign for the country park. Veer right at the fork and pass between sunny glades and picnic tables and benches. Follow the track to a kissing gate. Beyond them the track curves gradually to the left and then runs clear and straight to

Walk 43

WHAT TO LOOK FOR ℹ

As you cross the A34 Newbury bypass on leaving Bagnor, look across the fairways for a glimpse of **Donnington Grove** in the distance. Described by Pevsner as a 'little Gothic gem', this was the home of William Brummel, father of Beau the notorious regency dandy. The house was gothicised for him in about 1785. Beau fled to France after incurring heavy gambling debts and died in 1840.

a left curve. Pass a path on the right here and continue for a few paces to a bridleway.

② Turn sharp right and keep left at the next fork, avoiding a path on the extreme left. Keep to the right of a wooden seat and descend the bank between bracken. Cut through the trees at the bottom to a galvanised gate and follow the path ahead as it upgrades to a track. Pass **Honey Bottom Cottage** and go straight ahead when the track bends right. Follow the path along the woodland edge until you reach a wooden kissing gate on the right.

③ Head down the field slope towards Bagnor, with the path clearly defined by a row of waymarks. Make for a gate and follow the grassy path to the road. Turn left, pass the **Blackbird** inn and follow the track at the end of the car park. Go through the kissing gate and take the tarmac path up over the **A34** to a golf course. Keep left at the fork on the far side of the

WHERE TO EAT AND DRINK ℹ

Snelsmore Common Country Park is ideal for a picnic at the end of the walk. There are wooden tables and benches, enabling you to picnic in comfort amid the spacious grassy clearings. If you prefer a pub, the **Blackbird** at Bagnor offers a wide-ranging menu.

footbridge, heading towards woodland and an intersection. Cross the drive and follow a waymarked path on the right, threading through the trees. Keep the greens and fairways on the right. Emerge from the woodland at a gate and climb the slope to **Donnington Castle**.

④ Look for a gate behind it, leading to a track, and turn left. Pass between the timber barns of **Castle Farm** and bear left, down the tarmac bridleway. Re-cross the bypass and sweep right, following the drive as it dwindles to a track. Keep right at the fork and cut between fences. On the left are extensive fairways. Follow the track towards a house set against the trees and keep to the left of it.

WHILE YOU'RE THERE ℹ

If time allows, explore the heathland and woods of **Snelsmore Common Country Park**. The Newbury bypass protesters have finally decamped, but between May and September you are likely to see new residents in their place. Dexter cattle, one of the older breeds, have been introduced to the common to help control tree and scrub invasion.

⑤ Pass through a gate on to **Snelsmore Common** and go straight ahead at the waymarked junction. Pass beneath power lines and continue between bracken and gorse bushes. Keep right at the next fork and follow the waymark pointing towards the car park. A useful directional landmark is the fire control tower, seen on this stretch. Merge with another path at the next waymark and, within sight of the road and just before a stile, look for a galvanised gate on the left. Go through it and return to the car park.

Setting the Stage at Bagnor

An attractive extra loop on the delightful Lambourn Valley Way.
See map and information panel for Walk 43

•DISTANCE•	3 miles (4.8km)
•MINIMUM TIME•	1hr 30min
•ASCENT / GRADIENT•	82ft (25m) ▲ ▲ ▲
•LEVEL OF DIFFICULTY•	🚶 🚶 🚶

Walk 44 Directions
(Walk 43 option)

On reaching Bagnor (Point ③ on Walk 43), turn right along the main street, cross the **River Lambourn** and pass the entrance to the **Watermill Theatre**. A short walk along the drive reveals a striking view of the mill. This dates back to 1839 and was used to produce good quality writing paper before becoming a corn mill in the 1850s. The Watermill Theatre, which opened in 1965, has staged many prestigious productions over the years, earning well-deserved praise and plaudits from the arts world.

Continue along the road and take the next turning on the left. Follow the drive, part of the **Lambourn Valley Way**, and keep right at the entrance to **Bagnor Manor**. Pass a traffic mirror on the left and a bridleway on the right and continue ahead to a stile, Point Ⓐ.

Don't cross it, instead swing right and follow the way between hedgerows. Further on, the track curves gently to the right by a grove of trees. Step off the path for a few paces and you'll see, buried in the woodland, a graffiti-covered slab of the Berlin Wall, deposited here by the landowner, Lord Palumbo.

Eventually pass a stile on the right before the trail runs between trees. As you emerge from the woodland, swing left at the waymark and follow the path down to a stile and a bridge spanning the Lambourn. Cross over and veer right, taking the path by the meadow. Cross a weir and bridge to a stile and make for the dismantled **Lambourn Valley railway**. Make for another stile and go out to the road, Point Ⓑ.

Cross over and follow the byway ahead, keeping to the right of **Priddle's Farm**. After it bends left, pass the entrance to **Woodspeen Farm** and continue to the road on a bend. Swing left at this point to join a byway, following the muddy sunken path as it descends to **Snake Lane**. Bear left and walk to the road junction. Cross over and follow the waymarked lane, swinging right to a footbridge when you reach **Crossways Cottage**, Point Ⓒ.

Follow the riverside path. Cross a bridge to a stile and continue between fields and fences to the next stile. Continue ahead along the concrete drive and retrace your steps to the centre of **Bagnor**, rejoining Walk 43.

Walk 45

War and Peace at Greenham

Walk along a canal to a notorious common, returning to the start by train.

•DISTANCE•	7 miles (11.3km)
•MINIMUM TIME•	2hrs 45min
•ASCENT / GRADIENT•	Negligible ▲▲▲
•LEVEL OF DIFFICULTY•	林林 林林 林
•PATHS•	Canal tow path, tracks, common paths, roads, 1 stile
•LANDSCAPE•	Valley rising to wooded commons
•SUGGESTED MAP•	aqua3 OS Explorer 158 Newbury & Hungerford
•START / FINISH•	Grid reference: SU 527663
•DOG FRIENDLINESS•	On lead at Crookham and Greenham commons during breeding season, under control on canal tow path
•PARKING•	Thatcham Station
•PUBLIC TOILETS•	Newbury town and station

Walk 45 Directions

From **Thatcham Station** make for the **Kennet and Avon Canal**, a few paces to the south of the barrier, and turn right, signposted 'Ham Bridge'. Pass **Monkey Marsh Lock** and at the swing bridge, by a bridleway sign, turn left to **Chamberhouse Farm**. Pass between the sprawling farm outbuildings and follow the drive past the farmhouse and several cottages. The density of the buildings somehow conveys the impression that you are walking along the main street of a small village.

Cross the River Kennet and just beyond it the drive curves left. Keep right here and follow the track as it runs up through woodland to the road. Cross over to a gate leading on to **Crookham Common** and turn right. Follow the path parallel to the road, heading west. The television mast at Hannington and the ridge of Watership Down define the horizon.

Greenham Common's former airbase was once synonymous with CND rallies, women's protest groups and cruise missiles – a powerful evocation of the Cold War period and the threat of nuclear attack. But, today, the cruise missiles have gone, the derelict buildings have been demolished and the perimeter fence has been removed. At last new life is being breathed into Greenham Common, giving the site a softer, user-friendly image for the 21st century.

Originally an area of open common land, Greenham was acquired by the Air Ministry in 1941 for use as a military base, home to British

> **WHAT TO LOOK FOR** ⓘ
>
> The more acceptable 'churring' song of the **nightjar** has thankfully replaced the deafening roar of the American planes at Greenham Common. Listen out, too, for the songs of the **Dartford warbler** and the **woodlark**, among Britain's rarest birds. As Greenham Common continues to be transformed, so the wildlife gradually returns.

Walk 45

WHILE YOU'RE THERE ⓘ

If you've got the time, take a stroll through **Newbury** itself. There's plenty to see, including the Town Museum, housed in the 17th-century Cloth Hall, built to provide unemployed weavers with work. Next door to is the tourist information centre.

squadrons and then the United States Air Force. In 1951 the Americans set about building the longest military runway in Europe here and in the early 1980s the nuclear-armed cruise missiles arrived, making Greenham Common a focus of world attention. In its day, the airbase was virtually a self-contained American city, with everything from baseball pitches to its own school. The 1,000 acre (405ha) site even hosted international air shows and some local people feared that it might become the new London airport. Today the only sound you are likely to hear is that of birdsong. Thanks to a £7 million package, Greenham Common is at last being restored to its pre-Second World War state.

Follow the former taxiway, now a popular walk, and pass a hewn log at the side of the path, carved and sculpted to provide three welcome seats. On reaching the disused control tower, branch off to the right and pass a gate on the left, leading into the main car park. Follow the path towards a cattle grid on the road, veering left as you approach it towards some trees and bushes. Look for a gate in the fence, cross the road to a track and head down through the trees into **Bowdown Woods**, a nature reserve.

Pass **Bowdown Farm** and the fairways of **Newbury and Crookham Golf Course**. Beyond

the greens the chutes and conveyor belts of **Lower Farm Quarry** loom into view. A bird hide can also be seen here. Continue on the lane to a stile and gate and keep ahead, passing alongside the buildings of **Lower Farm. Newbury Racecourse** adjoins the route now, its striking grandstand can be seen in the distance. Pass under the railway and look for a swing bridge on the right, crossing the Kennet and Avon Canal. Once across, turn left and follow the tow path as far as **Ham Bridge**.

WHERE TO EAT AND DRINK ⓘ

The **Swan** is an ideal watering hole at the start and finish of the walk. Snacks and hot meals are available daily. Alternatively, pause for refreshment in Newbury where there is an excellent range of pubs, café bars and restaurants, including the **White Horse** close to the canal.

Cross over and follow the path along the south bank of the Kennet and Avon, making for **Ham Lock** at the confluence of the Kennet and the River Lambourn. Continue on a leafy stretch of tow path and cross over at the next footbridge, within sight of the **White House** pub. Keep to the path and cross the next bridge at the entrance to the marina. Pass **Greenham Lock** and walk ahead to the ring road. Pass under the road and alongside **Victoria Park** before reaching the next bridge. Leave the tow path, cross the canal into the wharf and keep right towards the tourist information centre and the **Market Place**. Bear left and head south, following **Cheap Street** to its right-hand bend. Continue ahead and then go round to the right for the **railway station** and a train back to Thatcham.

Farnborough's Old Rectory

Cross breezy downland to the former home of a fondly-remembered poet.

•DISTANCE•	7½ miles (12.1km)
•MINIMUM TIME•	3hrs
•ASCENT / GRADIENT•	150ft (46m) ▲▲▲
•LEVEL OF DIFFICULTY•	🚶 🚶 🚶
•PATHS•	Bridleways, field paths, tracks and quiet lanes, no stiles
•LANDSCAPE•	Remote downland country to south of Ridgeway
•SUGGESTED MAP•	aqua3 OS Explorer 170 Abingdon & Wantage
•START / FINISH•	Grid reference: SU 471825
•DOG FRIENDLINESS•	Under control across farmland
•PARKING•	Room to park in West Ilsley's main street
•PUBLIC TOILETS•	None on route

BACKGROUND TO THE WALK

John Betjeman (1906–84) has been described as the most popular poet of the 20th century. With his infectious laugh, air of eccentricity and sense of fun, he was an immensely popular character and, having been born into the television age, he was a natural performer for that particular medium. He loved the camera and it loved him in return.

Home on the Downs

Over the years Betjeman has been the subject of many distinguished television documentaries – intimate portraits that reflected the man's true identity and personality. They demonstrated his love for architecture, for historic landmarks and endangered buildings, illustrating to the viewer how he lovingly brought them to life in his own highly individual style.

However, few of these TV biographies make any mention of his home in the splendid Old Rectory at Farnborough in Berkshire. Betjeman and his wife Penelope moved here in 1945, and in the summer of that year she wrote to a friend, Wilhelmine Harrod: 'Father has bought us a beautiful William and Mary house 700ft up on the downs above Wantage with 12 acres of land, including a wood and two fields. It is a dream of beauty but has no water, no light and is falling down and needs six servants, so it will probably kill us in the end'.

Betjeman spent the war as a press attaché in Dublin, and when it was finally over, he and Penelope returned to their beloved Berkshire where they had begun their married life in 1934. He worked mainly in London, mixing with writers, poets and assorted Oxbridge intellectuals – select members of a precious coterie. But he was most at home in the peace and tranquillity of the countryside – especially the Vale of the White Horse, then still within Berkshire. Betjeman loved to explore the downs on foot, while Penelope galloped along the Ridgeway on Moti, her Arab mare.

An Inspiration

The Betjemans' love for this spectacular downland country remained undimmed when they moved to Farnborough. During the six years he lived in the village, Betjeman was typically productive in his work output. His collection of verse *New Bats in Old Belfries* was published in 1945, and in 1948 his *Selected Poems* won the Heinemann Award for Literature. At the same time, he worked on Murray's *Architectural Guide for Berkshire*, published in 1949.

The Betjemans moved to Wantage in 1951. It wasn't far away, and here he continued to indulge his love of the English countryside. In a TV interview in 1984, the year he died, Betjeman said that 'poetry makes life worth living', believing that the greatest thing he had done in his own life was to use his eyes and his feelings.

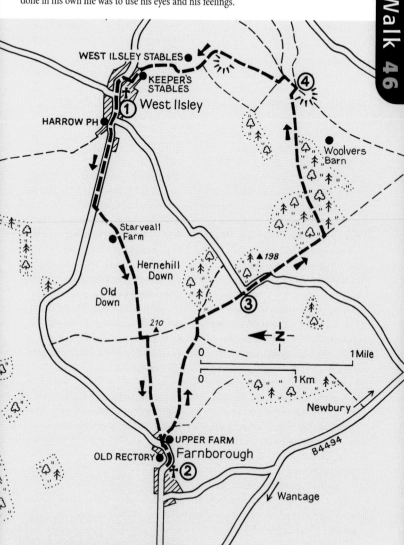

Walk 46 Directions

① Follow the road out of West Ilsley, heading west. Take the first bridleway on the left and make for a

gate. Continue ahead with the field boundary on your right. Bear left at the next junction, and then almost immediately right to follow the path across a large field. Look for a boundary corner ahead and keep

Walk 46

ahead in the next field, with the fence on your right. Follow the path across the field to the road by **Upper Farm**, veer left and walk along to Farnborough church and the **Old Rectory**.

② Walk back along the road to the farm, rejoin the track beside the outbuildings and look for a waymark and a pair of galvanised gates after about 60yds (55m). A field footpath and two tracks can be seen here. Keep right, directly alongside the farm. Cut between trees, bushes and margins of vegetation and cross a track further on. Continue ahead to a junction with a byway and bridleway. Keep going through woodland, following the **Ilsley Downs Riding Route**. Make for the next junction, where you can see a field beyond the trees, bear right and follow the clear path through the woods.

③ Keep right at the road and when it bends right, go straight on along a bridleway running across the fields towards trees. At length, the bridleway becomes a byway. Keep ahead when you reach a bend and walk along to a track on the left. Take it into the woodland and down the slope. As you approach a gap in the hedge, with a field seen ahead, veer right to follow a path running through the trees. Eventually it climbs gently to a junction. The walk turns left, but it

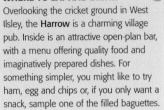

WHERE TO EAT AND DRINK
Overlooking the cricket ground in West Ilsley, the **Harrow** is a charming village pub. Inside is an attractive open-plan bar, with a menu offering quality food and imaginatively prepared dishes. For something simpler, you might like to try ham, egg and chips or, if you only want a snack, sample one of the filled baguettes.

is worth stepping to your right for several paces to admire the timeless view of Woolvers Barn and Woolvers Down.

④ Follow the byway, avoiding the public footpath on your right, and take the next bridleway on the left. Keep right at the next junction and cut between hedges. When the track bends left, there is a memorable view of West Ilsley sitting snug in its downland setting. Keep right at the next junction, following the track alongside **West Ilsley Stables**. Walk down to the road and turn left. As it bends right by a bridleway sign, go straight on by **Keeper's Stables**. Swing left as you reach the centre of **West Ilsley** and pass **All Saints Church**.

WHAT TO LOOK FOR
Once or twice on this walk, you'll come across **voluntary restraint signs**, requesting motorists not to indulge in off-road driving. Many cross-country routes have become fragile as a result of this activity and campaigners are attempting to stamp it out.

WHILE YOU'RE THERE
Make a point of looking at the west window in Farnborough's **All Saints Church**, dedicated to the memory of John Betjeman. The window, which depicts the tree of life, was designed by Betjeman's friend John Piper, executed by Joseph Nuttgens and placed here by the 'Friends of Friendless Churches'. Have a look at the village of **West Ilsley**, noted for its horse-racing connections and lines of pretty cottages. The church has a handwritten record of those who fell in the First and Second World Wars. Opposite the pub is a striking gazebo, erected by the villagers to mark the new millennium. Look out, too, for the attractively designed parish paths map.

Nags at Chaddleworth

Enjoy an exhilarating walk into Berkshire's renowned racing country.

•DISTANCE•	6 miles (9.7km)
•MINIMUM TIME•	2hrs 30min
•ASCENT / GRADIENT•	269ft (90m) ▲▲▲
•LEVEL OF DIFFICULTY•	👫 👫 👫
•PATHS•	Field paths and tracks, stretches of road, 8 stiles
•LANDSCAPE•	Classic farmland and remote, rolling country on edge of Lambourn Downs
•SUGGESTED MAP•	aqua3 OS Explorer 158 Newbury & Hungerford
•START / FINISH•	Grid reference: SU 416773
•DOG FRIENDLINESS•	On lead near livestock and in region of Whatcombe
•PARKING•	Permission given by landlord to park at Ibex pub
•PUBLIC TOILETS•	None on route

BACKGROUND TO THE WALK

The sweeping Lambourn Downs lie at the heart of Berkshire's loveliest and most isolated country – an area with a long tradition for racehorse training. Some of Britain's most famous winners have come from yards at Lambourn and West Ilsley and it is quite common to see strings of horses in the surrounding lanes.

The Sport of Kings

Horse racing dates back to the days of chariot races in Greece and Rome, with blockbuster movies like the immortal *Ben Hur* giving us a flavour of what it would have been like to vie for honours in the mammoth arena. Racing as we know it today has its origins in the period of the Stuart kings. James I established stables at Newmarket and it was here that he kept racehorses and 'riders for the races' – the first royal jockeys.

Towards the end of the 17th century racehorses were beginning to appear all over the country, with many breeders introducing Arabian stock. Three of these stallions were the sires from which all our thoroughbreds are descended. As the sport began to draw spectator interest, it split into two different categories – flat racing and racing over jumps.

Ideal Downs

Training stables were soon a permanent feature of life in the countryside, but they had to have easy access to large tracts of open downland and grassland over which gallops could be laid for racing practice. As the flinty, chalk soil made this landscape unsuitable for ploughing, the Lambourn Downs were considered ideal terrain for horses to compete with one another and jockeys to sharpen and hone their skills.

Prior to the 1840s horses were treated with little care or compassion. They were taken on long gallops and wrapped in thick rugs to make them sweat. More suitable methods of training were introduced, which enabled trainers to look at each horse individually and assess its potential, fitness level and merit as a future winner.

Take a walk on the Lambourn Downs and you'll find it's not just horses and their jockeys who frequent this breezy corner of Berkshire – walkers love it, too. But often you can go there and be completely alone. Other than occasional birdsong and the sound of trees sighing gently in the breeze, there is not a sound to be heard. There are no obvious indications of modern day life – few dwellings, roads or cars. It is difficult to imagine being more remote or cut off from civilisation than here in the quiet rural backwater of the Lambourn Downs – Berkshire's glorious racing country.

Walk 47 Directions

① From the **Ibex** take the path opposite the pub, emerging at the next road by **Box Hedge Cottage**. Keep right and follow the lane between cottages to some steps and a footpath on the right. The grassy path cuts between fields, towards houses. Keep to the right of the **village hall** and cross the next road to a kissing gate.

② Skirt the field, avoid a footpath on the left and continue walking straight ahead beside oak trees. On reaching a stile, cross over and keep a horse paddock on the left. Turn left at the next path junction and keep along the field edge. Eventually the path broadens out to a track. Go straight on at the road and just before it bends right, look for a waymarked track on the left, descending to the extensive buildings of **Manor Farm**.

WHILE YOU'RE THERE

Extend the walk around the village of **Chaddleworth**, with its charming cottages and period houses. The manor was given by William the Conqueror to Robert d'Oyley and it later belonged to the mother of Edward I. The church has a memorial to the Nelson family, a member of whom 'fought two dragoons in the Civil War and was never well afterwards', according to the church register. Listen out for the reassuring tick of the clock inside.

③ Cross the road and follow the path up the slope to a stile. Continue ahead, keeping the fence on your left, and make for the brow of the hill. Descend the field slope and make for some bushes in the field corner, concealing two stiles. Head straight down the next field, cross a stile and continue ahead in line with a row of telegraph poles towards the road. Cross a stile and head towards **Whatcombe** and **South Fawley**. Turn left at the entrance to Whatcombe and, on reaching the stud, keep left and take the waymarked bridleway.

④ Climb gradually, keeping to the right of some trees ahead. Make for a gateway into a plantation and cross the next field by cutting off the corner. If muddy, follow the left boundary. Look for a waymark in the trees, descend the bank to a path and turn left. On reaching a track, continue ahead, keeping to the left of farm outbuildings. Pass

to the right of **Henley Farm** and follow the byway down to some cottages by the road. Cross to a single track lane and bear left at the next junction.

⑤ Take the first lane on the right and climb steeply to a left-hand bend. Walk along to the next junction, turn right and pass the village sign for Chaddleworth. The church is on the left. Turn right towards **Great Shefford** and take the first left path. Look for an electricity transformer, enter a field via a squeeze stile and cross the field, keeping to the right of a large house and alongside a line of trees.

WHERE TO EAT AND DRINK

The **Ibex** at Chaddleworth, a Grade III listed building, was originally two cottages before becoming a bakery and an off-licence. In more recent years, the Ibex became famous throughout the racing world when, in the 1980s and early 1990s, it was run by the ex-jockey Colin Brown, who partnered the incomparable Desert Orchid for many years. Low ceilings and a cosy log fire add to the charm of the place. Expect a good selection of bar meals and a varied restaurant menu.

⑥ Cross a stile in the corner and turn left after a few paces at the public footpath sign. Follow the field boundary to the next waymark and drop down to a modern housing development. Turn right at the road and retrace your steps, back to the **Ibex**.

WHAT TO LOOK FOR

As you approach the buildings of Whatcombe, look for the striking bronze statue of **Snurge** who won the St Ledger in 1990. Whatcombe, one of the largest and most successful studs in the area, has produced several winners over the years. The farm stands on the site of a medieval village and there was once a 12th-century church here. When the church was demolished in the 16th century some of the carved stones were incorporated into the farm walls. Little remains of old Whatcombe, but a glance at the map reveals **Nun's Walk**, which was part of the road system when the village existed.

Combe Gibbet's Grisly Tale

Climb to Berkshire's windswept high ground, the scene of a 17th-century double murder.

•DISTANCE•	7 miles (11.3km)
•MINIMUM TIME•	3hrs
•ASCENT / GRADIENT•	560ft (171m) ▲▲▲
•LEVEL OF DIFFICULTY•	👥 👥 👥
•PATHS•	Woodland paths, field and downland tracks, some road and stretch of Wayfarer's Walk, 5 stiles
•LANDSCAPE•	Gentle farmland, steep scarp of Inkpen Hill and lofty heights of Wessex downs
•SUGGESTED MAP•	aqua3 OS Explorer 158 Newbury & Hungerford
•START / FINISH•	Grid reference: SU 379615
•DOG FRIENDLINESS•	Signs at intervals request dogs on leads
•PARKING•	Small car park to east of Walbury Hill
•PUBLIC TOILETS•	None on route

BACKGROUND TO THE WALK

Stand at the foot of Inkpen Hill on a bleak winter's afternoon and look for the outline of Combe Gibbet, just visible against the darkening sky. This has to be one of the wildest, most dramatic scenes in southern England. These lonely Wessex downs have a timeless quality to them and nowhere is this more apparent than here at Inkpen Hill.

Some years ago, I spent one sunny January afternoon attempting to photograph the gibbet from this same spot, dearly wanting to get the best picture for a lecture I was giving on walking in the area. I waited patiently as the sun finally slipped behind the escarpment, its golden glow illuminating the tall wooden post high on the downs. The camera caught it – thankfully. But, for me, the memory and effort of getting the best shot remained as vivid as the picture itself.

Crime Scene

The gibbet doesn't look much close up – but one has stood here for more than 325 years. The original gibbet was erected in 1676 following the conviction of a local labourer George Broomham and his mistress Dorothy Newman. The pair fell in love but their plans to be together were complicated by Broomham's wife Martha and his young son Robert.

The couple resorted to drastic measures to get rid of the boy and his mother – lying in wait for them on the crest of the hill. Eventually, Martha and Robert appeared on the scene, out for a walk on the downs. Broomham and Newman sprang an ambush, clubbing them to death with cudgels. It was a most vicious double murder – savage and utterly pointless.

Justice on a Gibbet

Thankfully, the pair were caught and appeared at Winchester Assizes in February 1676. Found guilty, it was decreed that they should be 'hanged in chaynes near the place of the murder'. The execution took place in March that year and it is said that the bodies could be seen hanging from several counties. Vandalism and the elements call for a new gibbet every so often, but successive structures over the years have ensured that the memory of that dreadful, needless incident is kept alive.

Not surprisingly, the events of that winter so long ago became the subject of a film, made in the late 1940s. Written and directed by Alan Cooke and John Schlesinger, who was then making his debut as a film director, *The Black Legend* captures the sense of isolation conveyed by this part of Berkshire. Local people were cast in the film which portrayed very effectively the horror of murder and violence in the midst of the English countryside.

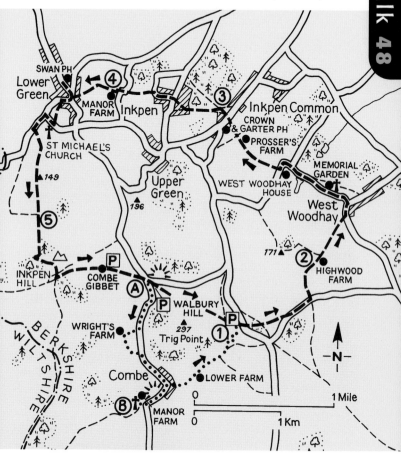

Walk 48 **Directions**

① Cross the road to a gate and go down the field towards the corner of a wood on the right. Edge round it and head for a curtain of trees ahead. Follow the path as it veers to the left of the woodland, making for a gate in the fence. Walk down the lane to a bridleway on the left.

Follow it between fields, sweeping right to **Highwood Farm**.

② Join a concrete track and follow it to the road. Turn left, keep left at the next junction and pass **St Laurence's Church**. Pass **West Woodhay House** and a turning for Kintbury and follow the road round a left bend. Turn right 80yds (73m) beyond it and continue to **Prosser's**

Farm. Keep ahead at the road, cross over and follow the track to a thatched cottage. Keep right at the first fork and then turn left when you get to the second.

③ Follow the woodland trail to a junction of paths by a stone and swing left. Keep to the path, skirting the woodland. Emerge from the trees, pass several houses and turn right at the first kissing gate. Follow the winding path across the field to a kissing gate. Cross the road to a lane and follow it down beside a gate and round to the right. Make for a gate on the left, pass a tennis court and walk ahead along the edge of a lawn to a kissing gate by an oak tree. Cross the field to another, keep left at the road towards **Manor Farm** and cross a stile in front of you at the bend.

WHAT TO LOOK FOR   ⓘ

Walbury Hill at 974ft (297m), just before the end of the walk, is the highest point in the county. Covering about |82 acres (33ha), it is also the largest Iron-Age fort in Berkshire. The gap in the south east corner of the fort is thought to be one of the original entrances. The small rounded mounds within the site are rabbit warrens constructed towards the end of the 19th century. Close to Combe Gibbet is a **plaque** commemorating the 9th Battalion of the Parachute Regiment who trained here for the assault into occupied France in 1944.

---

④ Veer left after a few paces to a gate. Follow a path between a hedge and fence, go through two kissing gates and follow a section of boardwalk. Look for a tree house on the right, pass alongside a beech hedge and follow a drive to the road. Bear left to a stile and follow the fence. Cross into the next field, towards Inkpen church and a stile. Turn right, down to the junction,

---

WHILE YOU'RE THERE   ⓘ

Stop to look at **St Laurence's Church** at West Woodhay. The church was built in 1883 and incorporates local flint and Bath stone in its construction. Relics from earlier churches on this site remain, among them some tiles that are preserved in the bell tower. The delightful garden next to the church was established by Mr Johnny Henderson of nearby West Woodhay House, in memory of his wife Sarah, whose tragic death at the age of 47 was the result of a riding accident.

---

bear left, pass the Inkpen village sign and swing left to follow a waymarked track. Continue to the next waymark and then keep a line of trees and bushes on the right before heading out across open fields. Make for the next waymark and keep ahead between the trees.

⑤ The path climbs gradually to reach a stile. Aim diagonally left, ascending steeply now towards a cleft in the ridge of **Inkpen Hill**. At the summit, look for a gate in the field boundary and keep the fence on your right. Make for a gate ahead and turn left to join a byway. Follow the track to **Combe Gibbet** and cross two stiles at either end of it. Continue down the track to the road, cross over and follow the **Wayfarer's Walk**. Keep on the main track, back to the car park.

WHERE TO EAT AND DRINK   ⓘ

The **Swan** at Lower Green is one of West Berkshire's most popular pubs offering well-presented dishes. Next door is a shop selling organic produce where you can stock up before leaving. The **Crown and Garter** at Inkpen Common is also popular and serves a good range of food and drink. Reputedly, this is where the bodies of Broomham and his mistress were kept before burial.

Combe – Berkshire's Secret Village

Head south from the ridge of Inkpen Hill, making for a tiny settlement hidden below the downs.
See map and information panel for Walk 48

•DISTANCE•	8½ miles (13.7km)
•MINIMUM TIME•	4hrs
•ASCENT / GRADIENT•	725ft (221m) ▲▲▲
•LEVEL OF DIFFICULTY•	🚶🚶🚶

Walk 49 Directions
(Walk 48 option)

At Point Ⓐ, from the car park at the start of the **Wayfarer's Walk**, follow the lane as it twists and turns down the hill towards Combe. Turn right at the entrance to **Wright's Farm** and walk along to the farmhouse and outbuildings. Bear left at the waymark and follow the track as it curves back to the road. Turn right to the village of **Combe**, follow the road round to the right and walk along **Church Lane** to reach **St Swithin's Church**, its entrance hidden from view to the left of **Manor Farm**.

To the right of the entrance to the house is a field with a fine view of the gibbet seen against the skyline. Walbury Hill (974ft/297m), the highest chalk summit in Britain, can be seen from here, blending with the ridge of the downs.

There is no quick or easy way of reaching Berkshire's loneliest village, but that's how it residents like it. St Swithin's Church, in a charming, tree-shaded setting, is one of the county's hidden delights – miles from busy roads and thankfully removed from the hurly burly of the modern world. Work on the church here first began in 1160. The little building has flint walls, a timber tower and a porch dating back to 1652. St Swithin's was restored in 1934, largely through the efforts of a former rector here, the Revd William Hibwood Mowat.

Return to the centre of the village, Point Ⓑ, and turn right for **Lower Farm**. Pass a post box and a footpath on the right and keep ahead on the track. Follow the waymarked byway on reaching the buildings of Lower Farm, the track climbing steadily between trees now. Continue ahead at the right-hand bend, passing through a galvanised gate. Follow the bridleway to a fork and veer left to join a sunken path. Over to your left the buildings of Combe can be seen nestling snugly below. Continue to the next fork and keep right. Climb up above clumps of gorse bushes and look for a gate and waymark in the fence corner. Beyond is the car park where both Walks 48 and 49 finish.

Walk 50

Enborne and Britain's Second Line of Defence

Follow the pretty Kennet and Avon Canal to Hamstead Park.

•DISTANCE•	4 miles (6.4km)
•MINIMUM TIME•	1hr 30min
•ASCENT / GRADIENT•	90ft (27m) ▲ ▲ ▲
•LEVEL OF DIFFICULTY•	🚶🚶 🚶🚶 🚶🚶
•PATHS•	Tracks, roads, estate drives and canal tow path, 1 stile
•LANDSCAPE•	Lowland country bisected by Kennet and Avon Canal, elegant parkland on south side of Kennet Valley
•SUGGESTED MAP•	aqua3 OS Explorer 158 Newbury & Hungerford
•START / FINISH•	Grid reference: SU 435657
•DOG FRIENDLINESS•	Under control on canal tow path, on lead in Hamstead Park
•PARKING•	Car park by Enborne church
•PUBLIC TOILETS•	None on route

Walk 50 Directions

From the car park by the church, turn right and follow the road towards Newbury. Pass **Church Lane** and, as the road descends a gentle slope, the buildings of Newbury edge into view in the distance. Take the next signposted footpath on the left, at the entrance to **Step Up Cottage**, and as the drive sweeps left, continue straight on along the track beside **Enborne Copse**. Follow it across open fields and soon the **Kennet and Avon Canal** comes into view ahead. Once over the bridge, turn left by a pill box and go down to the tow path.

Completed in 1810, the 87 mile (140km) long Kennet and Avon Canal took 16 years to construct. The final bill was in the region of £1 million. With 104 locks and many other impressive features, the canal is regarded as a triumph of engineering.

The Kennet and Avon was built to provide a direct trade link between London and Bristol, thus avoiding the treacherous south coast route which took ships around Land's End. The canal eventually became redundant in the late 1940s but dedicated armies of supporters were determined not to let it die. Restored over many years, the canal was eventually re-opened by the Queen at Devizes in 1990.

Since then it has become one of the south's most colourful and vibrant waterways. But 60 years ago it

---

> **WHAT TO LOOK FOR** ⓘ
>
> Sir William Craven built a magnificent mansion at **Hamstead Park** in 1660, but the house was tragically destroyed by fire and all that remains of it are several sets of crumbling gate piers and some overgrown castle mounds. Said to have been modelled on Heidelberg Castle in Germany, Hamstead Park was designed by the eminent Dutch architect Sir Balthazar Gerbier.

would have been a very different story. Follow the canal tow path and you'll spot ugly brick and concrete pill boxes strategically placed at intervals along the bank. Unsightly though they undoubtedly are, they are vivid reminders of the Second World War and the time when Britain braced itself for invasion.

WHERE TO EAT AND DRINK

A few minutes' walk from the route, towards the A4, lies the **Red House** at Marsh Benham, offering a quality, up-market restaurant and bar menu with such dishes as slow roasted leg of duck, roast fillet of salmon and chargrilled rib-eye steak. The Red House is closed on Sunday evening and all day on Monday.

Cutting a swathe across England from east to west, the waterway was to act as the second line of defence if the Germans had breached the south coast blockade. Tank traps were laid to deter the enemy from making deeper inroads and concrete machine gun posts were positioned along the tow path to guard the open, undefended country to the south.

Head west, passing **Benham Lock**. Pass a tributary stream running into some woods. The railway line, transporting speeding inter-city trains as well as local services, is seen on the right along this stretch. A little further on, at **Benham Broad**, the natural river and the canal unite. Cross the weir by the footbridge and continue on the tow path, passing a cottage on the opposite bank. A line of poplar trees and the buildings of **Marsh Benham** edge nearer. Join the road at the next bridge, turn left, cross the Kennet and pass **Hamstead Mill**, formerly a model mill belonging to the Craven estate.

Avoid a drive on the left, just beyond the mill, and continue on the road, following it alongside a brick wall. When the road curves right, continue ahead on a footpath leading to **Hamstead church**. Originally Norman, St Mary's occupies a delightful corner of Hamstead Park, its brick tower looking out across the Kennet Valley. In the corner of the churchyard is a mausoleum containing the Craven family vault. Keep the church on the right, make for a gate ahead and turn left, following the grassy track as it bends left and descends between trees to a drive and waymark.

Turn right, following it through a stately landscape dotted with oak and beech trees. This is **Hamstead Park**. Pass over a cattle grid and keep to the drive as it sweeps to the right, with the parkland estate extending to distant horizons. Follow the drive as it curves left, pass a turning on the left and as the drive sweeps right towards a gate and bungalow, go straight on along a path to an avenue of beech and horse chestnut trees. On the right is the former home of the Craven family, which later became a nursing home. Turn left and walk along the drive, following it as it curves left. Make for a gate and a cattle grid, cross a stile and exit to the road. Opposite is the car park where the walk began.

WHILE YOU'RE THERE

Have a look at the historic 12th-century **Enborne church** located at the start and finish of the walk. The church, built on land once owned by Romsey Abbey, has a Saxon font decorated with emblems of the Passion, a fresco painted by an Italian monk from nearby Sandleford Priory and a bell cast in 1260.

Walking in Safety

All these walks are suitable for any reasonably fit person, but less experienced walkers should try the easier walks first. Route finding is usually straightforward, but you will find that an Ordnance Survey map is a useful addition to the route maps and descriptions.

Risks

Although each walk here has been researched with a view to minimising the risks to the walkers who follow its route, no walk in the countryside can be considered to be completely free from risk. Walking in the outdoors will always require a degree of common sense and judgement to ensure that it is as safe as possible.

- Be particularly careful on cliff paths and in upland terrain, where the consequences of a slip can be very serious.

- Remember to check tidal conditions before walking on the seashore.

- Some sections of route are by, or cross, busy roads. Take care and remember traffic is a danger even on minor country lanes.

- Be careful around farmyard machinery and livestock, especially if you have children with you.

- Be aware of the consequences of changes in the weather and check the forecast before you set out. Carry spare clothing and a torch if you are walking in the winter months. Remember the weather can change very quickly at any time of the year, and in moorland and heathland areas, mist and fog can make route finding much harder. Don't set out in these conditions unless you are confident of your navigation skills in poor visibility. In summer remember to take account of the heat and sun; wear a hat and carry spare water.

- On walks away from centres of population you should carry a whistle and survival bag. If you do have an accident requiring the emergency services, make a note of your position as accurately as possible and dial 999.

Acknowledgements

From the author:
My grateful thanks to the staff of Bletchley Park, the Buckinghamshire Railway Centre, Hartwell House Hotel, Old Jordans, Hughenden Manor, Stoke Poges Memorial Gardens, Dorney Court, Dinton Pastures Country Park, Ludgrove School, the West Berkshire Brewery, West Berkshire Council and the various libraries in both Berkshire and Buckinghamshire.

AA Publishing and Outcrop Publishing Services would like to thank Chartech for supplying aqua3 maps for this book. For more information visit their website: www.aqua3.com.

Series management: Outcrop Publishing Services Ltd, Cumbria
Series editor: Chris Bagshaw
Front cover: World Pictures Limited